Brilliant, clear, and cogent! Gve and important case that exce   t West, shame has been consid   n, signaling that we have lost standing in the community. In the age of social media, where our lives are more exposed than ever, Ten Elshof shows us that the journey out of shame cannot be made by an individual alone but depends on a community of others who will help bring the person honor.

KEN SHIGEMATSU, pastor and author of *God in My Everything* and *Survival Guide for the Soul*

With many clear examples, Ten Elshof does an outstanding job of sorting out the many meanings of shame. He clarifies the important issue of when shame is a healthy emotion that communities should encourage and when it is not. One might think that shame is not an important topic today until, as Ten Elshof points out, we consider how much our culture celebrates shamelessness and at the same time increasingly allows shaming.

GEORGE MARSDEN, professor emeritus, University of Notre Dame

In *For Shame*, Gregg Ten Elshof provides readers with new eyes to see a recently disparaged but important dimension of human psychology that is tied to social reality. With his characteristic combination of careful analysis and life-enriching wisdom, he clarifies the true nature of shame and its valuable role in human flourishing. In doing so, he offers a timely and prophetic corrective—both to current efforts in our individualistic society to eliminate shame from our lives altogether and to the increasingly prevalent but destructive practice of shaming other people. With sensitivity to the nuances of the human condition and an artful use of examples and stories to illustrate human experience, Ten Elshof helps readers see the essential contribution of shame to a life well lived. Readers will gain a fresh and fruitful perspective on themselves, the society in which we live, and the gospel that takes away the shame of our sin.

It's an honor for me to recommend *For Shame* as a thorough and fair-minded case—for shame.

JIM TAYLOR, professor of philosophy and
department chair, Westmont College

In a culture that is suspicious of shame but accepting of shaming, Gregg Ten Elshof makes a powerful case that we've gotten things exactly backward. This work places shame (and shamelessness) in the context of rival views of human flourishing and the history of philosophy, East and West. This book also takes empirical research in psychology seriously but not uncritically. His reinterpretation of the story of the prodigal son as a rescuing from shame is deeply illuminative. Clearly written, free of technical jargon, and biblically informed, Ten Elshof's absolutely terrific exploration of shame deserves wide readership.

CHRISTOPHER KACZOR, author of *The Gospel of Happiness*
and coauthor of *Jordan Peterson, God, and Christianity*

With examples from life, philosophical analysis, biblical stories, and humor, Ten Elshof argues that there is a narrow band of appropriate feelings of shame that are actually positive. He points out that most of us want to be well-regarded in a community of others we respect, feeling honored rather than feeling shame, and this urge to avoid feeling shame can contribute to the good of our communities. However, he cautions against the shaming of others and urges societal changes that would actively honor those who feel ashamed or less than others for no valid reason, for example due to their ethnicity, gender, disability, or circumstance beyond their control. Counselors, psychologists, pastors, chaplains, and spiritual directors would find this book useful. His critique of the research on shame and his careful distinctions between shame and other feelings such as guilt, low self-esteem, and self-hatred should aid future researchers and help all of us who look to apply that research and subsequent interpretations to our lives and the lives of those we care for.

LYNN UNDERWOOD, author of *Spiritual Connection in Daily Life*

FOR SHAME

FOR SHAME

Rediscovering the Virtues of a Maligned Emotion

GREGG A. TEN ELSHOF

ZONDERVAN
REFLECTIVE

ZONDERVAN REFLECTIVE

For Shame
Copyright © 2021 by Gregg A. Ten Elshof

Requests for information should be addressed to:
Zondervan, 3900 Sparks Dr. SE, Grand Rapids, Michigan 49546

Zondervan titles may be purchased in bulk for educational, business,
fundraising, or sales promotional use. For information, please email
SpecialMarkets@Zondervan.com.

ISBN 978-0-310-10866-5 (softcover)
ISBN 978-0-310-10868-9 (audio)
ISBN 978-0-310-10867-2 (ebook)

Cover Design: Thinkpen Design
Cover Image: © Olly / Shutterstock
Interior Design: Denise Froehlich

Printed in the United States of America

21 22 23 24 25 /TRM/ 10 9 8 7 6 5 4 3 2 1

To whom can you dedicate a book about shame? I have this problem a lot. When you write about things like self-deception and shame, nobody wants to see their name in your books. I can think of only one person in my life upon whom can safely be conferred this dubious honor.

As we'll see in the pages to follow, the opposite of shame is not self-respect, self-validation, or healthy self-esteem. The opposite of shame is honor. And honor is not something you can effectively give yourself. In the typical case, honor requires that someone with social capital to spare condescends to identify strongly with you. It often requires that someone above your station in life risks the social decline that will be theirs if they make public their strong affiliation with you. That is what Laurel did for me in July 1993. I have never been so honored as I was on that summer day. And since that day, I have enjoyed unceasingly the most powerful safeguard against the potentially destructive effects of shame. I have enjoyed, that is, the dignity of being known, accepted, and celebrated. Even insofar as I have known the painful experience of shame, it has always been offset by the honor of Laurel's embrace. There are no words to express my gratitude for this gift, this mercy.

To Laurel

CONTENTS

FOREWORD

Shame has the power to drive and deter human behavior. It is a subject of study across many academic disciplines, with countless books and articles published on the topic. Yet despite all this, a shroud of mystery still cloaks our understanding of shame. Consider that even though several writers may use the same word—*shame*—at times it feels like they are talking about different things entirely. Popular speakers such as Brené Brown bemoan the destructive presence of shame in our lives. Others, such as Confucius, laud it as an essential tool for shaping right character. So why can't we all get on the same page?

This, I think, is where this book can help us. Let's be clear—few people could have written a book like this, yet Gregg Ten Elshof, a philosopher focused squarely on the human experience, is superbly equipped for the task. Ten Elshof has spent decades reflecting on psychology, spiritual formation, culture, and worldview. *For Shame* is a fitting title because this book is an *apology* for shame—an attempt to defend shame. Still, you might ask, "Why do we *need* to defend shame?"

One of the problems Ten Elshof notes is that in recent

years, a flurry of books and songs have espoused the benefits of being "unashamed" or "shameless." But when did being shameless become a virtue, something to be praised? Don't dismiss my question with an, "Okay, boomer," because the fact remains that for much of the world, being "shameless" remains one of the ugliest insults you can give a person. Ten Elshof helpfully asks us to rethink what living in a shameless culture would look like (if it were even possible). As it turns out, getting rid of shame is far less appealing than some have suggested.

As a philosopher, Ten Elshof knows that not everyone is going to agree with what he says. Topics like shame and honor stir controversy, especially when discussing them in the context of the Bible and the Christian life. But this doesn't scare Ten Elshof, and *For Shame* wrestles with tough issues and makes provocative claims, though the goal is always constructive.

One of the first steps in making progress is clarifying our terms, so Ten Elshof leads us to consider *what* we mean by shame, and he efficiently but effectively defines several key ideas related to shame. But make no mistake, *For Shame* is far more than a dry, dictionary-like parsing of terms. It is filled with concrete examples and illustrations drawn from a wide breadth of literature on shame and honor, giving us a balanced and carefully nuanced perspective.

I was excited when I first heard that Gregg was writing this book, knowing the unique perspective he would provide for readers—and I have not been disappointed. This is a timely book with plentiful and profound insights. Some may think an entire book on shame sounds depressing, but this isn't a negative or discouraging book. It's a book about human flourishing, and as surprising as it may sound, a proper understanding of shame can contribute in positive ways to healthy, human flourishing.

I challenge you to reflect deeply on these proposals. Invite others into this conversation. Even if your initial instinct is to dismiss some of Ten Elshof's ideas, take a moment to pause. This is the work of a thoughtful scholar, and this is a carefully written book. Take the time to understand the argument and why it matters.

Jackson Wu
Theologian-in-Residence, Mission One
Phoenix, Arizona, USA

CHAPTER 1
APOLOGY

Not long ago, I was on a solo backpack trip through the San Jacinto Wilderness. Backpacking in such beautiful country, while glorious, presents the would-be practitioner with many challenges—among them, the biological need to digest food and discard waste in an environmentally sensitive way that respects the dignity of others on the trail. This involves preparing in advance with materials and strategies for responsible "bathroom" stops. Seasoned backpackers know all about this, and there's no reason to get into the gory details here. Suffice it to say that on the present occasion, I was suitably prepared and had deployed the relevant strategies.

Nevertheless, I was discovered at exactly the wrong time by another hiker who had wandered significantly off-trail. The interpersonal contact was brief and, I dare say, profoundly uncomfortable for us both. I can't say for certain what the other hiker felt. But I know how I felt. Though I had done nothing wrong, I felt wrongly situated in the world. I felt as though my very presence (such as it currently was) was a source of pain, discomfort, and embarrassment both for this other person and for me. I felt a significant downtick in my social standing in the world—like I was a less respectable person than I had been just moments before. I felt like a person of slightly lesser consequence. I wanted to shrink, to disappear. I think the other hiker felt similarly. Though he had done nothing wrong, I think he felt wrongly situated in the world. He felt his own existence as a cause of pain, discomfort, and embarrassment in the world. He felt slightly less respectable than he did just moments before. He also wanted to shrink, to disappear. Thankfully, he *did* disappear in relatively short order, and the experience faded into the background of an otherwise sublime experience in the wilderness.

The emotion I'm describing is, I think, a familiar one. We've all experienced it. Nobody I know likes it. Sometimes it is mercifully short-lived and relatively mild in its intensity (as was the case in my hiking experience). But sometimes it persists because the conditions that give it occasion are not so easily eliminated. Often, parties to this emotional experience cannot simply disappear as did the other hiker. And sometimes the feeling occurs with an intensity that drowns out nearly all else.

On some occasions, the emotion arises in connection with something we've done that we know (or think) to be wrong. We suffer the embarrassment of social discrediting and we want to shrink or hide when we are caught (or when we imagine being caught) in serious moral failure. In these cases, an experience of guilt typically accompanies the emotion in question. On other occasions, though, guilt does not accompany the experience of this emotion. I may experience this kind of embarrassed social discrediting, for example, if my parent is caught in a serious moral failure or if someone accidentally sees me naked. Folks with publicly discernible impairments or disabilities often report feeling this way in connection with the real or imagined public experience of their disability. Sometimes folks experience this felt loss of social standing as a consequence of being significantly wronged by others. Victims of sexual abuse and discrimination of all sorts are paradigmatic cases in point. The emotion in question, it seems, accompanies many of these experiences for reasons having nothing to do with wrongdoing on the part of the people who have them.

The emotion that runs through all these cases—from the trivial and easily shrugged-off to the profoundly painful and potentially life-disruptive—is shame.

When we suffer shame, we feel somehow wrongly situated in the world. Guilt often accompanies this experience. But the experience of shame always involves the sense of diminished social standing—the experience of losing significance in the company of respected others (actual or merely imagined). We experience ourselves as a source of pain, discomfort, inconvenience, or embarrassment for ourselves and for others. For this reason, shame usually causes the desire to shrink, to hide, or to disappear altogether. This feeling of diminished social consequence will be less acutely experienced, it might seem, if we can find our way free of the real or imagined gaze of the other—if we can find the sweet relief of isolation.

Often, though, what health and healing require in circumstances that give rise to shame is the knowing and accepting embrace of the other. We need to be *seen* when we're wrongly situated and accepted *precisely in that condition* to be free of our felt loss of social standing when we experience shame. But shame often motivates the pursuit of isolation. We often desire to escape the gaze of the other (or, worse, to do violence to the other in such a way as to eliminate the possibility of their gaze). The experience of shame, then, often pulls us *away* from health and healing. For this reason, shame has been the cause of much dysfunction and harm in human experience. So it is no surprise that much contemporary writing on shame has as its ostensible goal the denigration of shame or even the eradication of shame from the range of felt human emotions.

The central thesis of this book is that the wholesale denigration of shame and the corresponding attempt to eradicate it is misguided. This book is a *defense* of shame—an attempt to articulate how shame contributes to a healthy moral and emotional experience.

I wish to begin with apology—both in the popular sense (as an attempt to make reparation for pain I've caused or am about to cause) and in the older, more academic sense (the giving of reasons for a particular belief, conviction, or undertaking). First, I wish to apologize at the front end for what some readers might initially find hurtful about the aim of this project—defending shame. For many people, shame is a destructive and health-disrupting force. Many need to be rescued from the shame that has crippled them for years. And for those whose lives have been undone by shame, the suggestion that this emotion has an important role to play in human experience may itself be a cause of significant pain. My hope is that the following comments here at the outset will partly assuage whatever pain this book causes.

First, though I look at the need to redeem some of the healthy aspects of shame, not all shame is healthy. Much shame is destructive, and it would have been better were it never felt or experienced. Many of the books and resources that denigrate shame and seek to eradicate it have brought unmistakable healing. Countless people have found their way free of destructive and health-disrupting shame with the help of these resources. This is cause for celebration. Even as I criticize the wholesale denigration of shame, I want to celebrate any occasion when one finds their way free of debilitating or unhealthy shame.

The situation we're in with shame is analogous to the one we're in with sexuality. For many people, sexuality has been a destructive and health-disrupting force in their lives. Whether through abuse or dysfunction, they have experienced harm and need to be rescued and redeemed from the destructive effects of sexuality in their lives. When something has powerfully damaged us, it's tempting to eradicate it. But this current situation is a case of swinging the pendulum too far in the other direction. A full account of human sexuality must include both the ways we use it to harm ourselves and others *and* an articulation of its positive contributions to human experience. Yes, we must seek to be sensitive to those who have been harmed by negative experiences surrounding sexuality. Yet a full-orbed perspective on human sexuality and human flourishing takes into account both the negative and the positive. The potential for destructive abuse and dysfunction is great, to be sure. But we cannot let it narrow our vision to the point where we miss the positive aspects. I think something like this is true of shame. There is a relatively narrow band of "shame experience" that makes an important and positive contribution to human life. And there is a seemingly infinite field of potentially harmful abuse and dysfunction. Resources abound, at present, for dealing with and finding freedom from shame. But the full story about shame requires an articulation of its unique contribution to human flourishing. And precious few are the resources aimed at making clear the positive contribution that shame makes to our life together.

This brings me to the second type of apology I wish to make—setting forth the reasons for this undertaking. I attempt to defend the legitimacy and fruitfulness of shame and to clarify its contribution to the good life. But why? Even if there *is* a narrow band of healthy shame experience, why bother? If, by and large, shame has been a destructive force in human experience, why not simply be rid of it? It's easy to see why we would want to temper our critique of unhealthy sexuality with a positive vision for healthy sexual experience. The thought of a sex-less world is hardly a utopia. But would a world devoid of shame really be all that bad? What would be lost? Anything we care about?

I hope to make clear that something good would be lost were shame to be eradicated from the range of felt human emotion. While much of contemporary literature is aimed at helping folks who experience unhealthy and debilitating shame, this book seeks to address a *different* problem—the problem of an increasingly *shameless* culture. Chapter 1 will unpack what we mean when we talk about shamelessness, but for now you might ask yourself, "Is 'shamelessness' a vice or a virtue?" Most people I've talked with don't find it complimentary to be described (or to have something they've done be described) as "shameless." Why is that?

Shamelessness—or the lack of a sense of shame—is on the rise. It is most evident in the arenas of politics and the entertainment industry. But it is also increasingly present in the rough and tumble of everyday life—in the classroom, at the family dinner table, and in the workplace. And I will argue that this *lack* of shame has a destructive effect on our life together. Shamelessness is the tendency not to feel shame where shame would be the apt thing to feel. If shamelessness is a vice—not a virtue—then there are conditions and circumstances wherein shame is the appropriate emotional response. The first step in addressing the rise of shamelessness in our culture is to clarify what those conditions and circumstances are and to determine the appropriate contours of this particular emotion. So the first and most straightforward reason for this defense of shame is to address the disintegrating effects of the rise of shamelessness in modern society.

Overview

We begin by examining shamelessness more closely. What are the conditions under which we would describe someone as "shameless"? And what exactly is the failure we attribute to someone who is "shameless"? The next order of business is to distinguish shame from the closely related experience of guilt. Though these two emotions often accompany each other, they needn't. We will consider instances where shame is experienced in the absence of guilt and where guilt is experienced in the absence of shame.

Having clarified the nature of shame, we will take a brief look backward to examine the place of shame in a healthy life, drawing from some of the culture-making wisdom traditions in human history. A common misperception is that the East is a shame-and-honor culture and that Western moral sentiment has been rather more guilt-centric. The truth is that shame has been an important moral emotion in both the East and the West. It is only in the *post-Enlightenment* West that shame has had trouble finding a natural home. The radical individualism of our contemporary Western mindset renders us *uniquely* incapable of integrating shame, unlike virtually all other cultures around the globe and throughout human history.

The reality that shame has been universally embraced across human cultures, both in the East and West, should give us pause. At the very least, it should make us question whether our contemporary denigration of shame is missing something others have seen and valued. On the other hand, sometimes a new movement in culture at a particular time and place represents a genuine improvement over what has been nearly universally accepted in the past. Recent movements against slavery, racism, and gendered hierarchies are plausible examples of this. So it's possible that the negative view of shame that accompanies contemporary Western individualism represents a genuine improvement in the human condition. Perhaps we are healthier without shame and should be grateful for this unique insight and contribution of contemporary Western culture. Perhaps radical individualism, whatever its other merits or demerits, should be lauded for the denigration and wholesale rejection of shame.

An impressive body of empirical psychological research certainly seems to indicate that shame correlates with unhealthy states and postures (e.g., suicide, eating disorders, anxiety, and depression), while guilt does not. Any defense of the idea that shame has a positive role to play in human experience must grapple with this impressive case against shame. Defending shame in light of this research requires careful attention to the subtle differences between shame, low self-esteem, self-loathing, and other failures of self-respect that routinely disrupt health and well-being. I hope to advocate a mediating posture that takes the research seriously, carefully distinguishing healthy shame from the unhealthy emotional and cognitive attitudes that sometimes follow in its wake.

Once we have *healthy* shame squarely in view, we'll be well positioned to ask whether shame has work to do that can't be done equally well in some other way. Suppose it has not been demonstrated that *healthy* shame is maladaptive. Even so, if guilt can do for human experience everything that shame can do, why bother with the seemingly more dangerous and potentially destructive experience of shame? A defense of shame must show that there is important work for shame to do that cannot be done by guilt.

Finally, having made the case that we should preserve shame in some way because it contributes to the good life, I want to distinguish between shame and *shaming*. It's a short step from the suggestion that shame has important work to do to the idea that we are warranted in shaming others—something all too easily accomplished in the wake of the social media revolution of the last decade. But seeing the good of shame should not lead us to shame others. This is not a step we should take. We will explore the difference between shame and shaming and the possibility that shame can do its good work without the need for self-appointed shame dispensers.

Again, I wish to be clear. Shame is a difficult and painful topic. This makes it difficult for me to know what to hope for you as you make your way through this book. I do, of course, hope the book will be helpful—that it will play some small part in stemming the tide against the rise of shamelessness. I also hope it will be, at least in some places, enjoyable.

And if you find it neither enjoyable nor helpful? Well . . . shame on you.

CHAPTER 2
SHAMELESS

S teve went to Harvard.

That was twenty-three years ago. Still, if you've known Steve for more than ten minutes, you know that he went to Harvard. Steve has an uncanny ability to insert his Harvard-alumni status into a conversation about anything. Recently a conversation about donuts (*donuts!*) turned into a discussion of a donut shop in Harvard Square that had unparalleled bear claws. Steve wondered aloud whether that donut shop he frequented as a student was still there. Those of us who have known Steve for a long time always feel a little uncomfortable on his behalf when the conversation takes one of these forced and predictable turns. We can read the faces of the others in the room. We cringe when we see their mildly disgusted reactions to the shameless self-promotion on display. But not Steve. He feels no discomfort at all. He is unaffected by the embarrassed sideways and downward glances of his conversation partners. He can't feel the air flying out of the discussion as fewer and fewer make the attempt to contribute to it and more and more seize on any available escape to another conversation or occupation.

To his ear, these forced references to his alma mater fit hand in glove with whatever we happen to be talking about.

Steve is a *shameless* self-promoter. But what do we mean, exactly, when we put him in that category? Has he done anything wrong? Anything immoral? Nothing obvious. No one is wronged when Steve self-promotes in the way he often does. No one is harmed. There are no rights violations. But something is wrong with Steve. He doesn't feel something that, it seems, healthy, well-functioning people feel when they get caught up in self-promotion. It should be uncomfortable for him to lose social status the way he so obviously does when he makes these ceaseless references to Harvard. But it isn't. Steve is shameless.

Notice that it is *not* the act of self-promotion itself that warrants the indictment of shamelessness. There is a difference, after all, between a shameless self-promoter and someone who self-promotes. The difference lies in the presence or absence of shame that we expect to naturally accompany self-promotion when all is otherwise well in the human psyche.

Consider Janet, an author who has been gaining some notoriety for her past two books. She recognizes that she has a growing audience and wishes to leverage her newfound influence to help folks who reside in homeless communities not far from where she lives. She's just completed a third book—an autobiography—and has instructed the publisher to direct all proceeds to various dimensions of aid in the alleviation of suffering for these homeless communities. She'd like the book to succeed since she wants to help these people as much as possible. So she's been on tour for the book. She routinely calls attention to the book, extolling its virtues and encouraging others to pay attention to what she has written. She consciously and frequently tries to turn conversations to her book to make folks aware of its existence. And, since the book is an autobiography, she constantly talks about herself. But she is regularly plagued with a kind of discomfort about the whole business. She's profoundly uncomfortable talking about herself and her work as much as she has been. Janet is caught up in self-promotion. But she is not shameless.

Janet will often begin a conversational reference to her book with a lighthearted and self-deprecating apology for a "shameless plug" for her book. Ironically, her self-referential accusation of shamelessness is an indication that she is not shameless at all. It is instead an attempt to assuage the feeling of shame that, for Janet, invariably accompanies these acts of self-promotion. That she deploys conversational strategies to lessen her experience of shame is evidence of the shame she experiences. Janet is a self-promoter. But she is not a shameless self-promoter.

Consider one more example. Like Steve and Janet, Phil routinely turns the focus of conversations toward himself. But unlike Janet, Phil can point to no laudable end served by his endless self-promotion. Phil didn't get much affirmation from his parents and has spent most of his adult life finding ways in conversation to fill that void. Phil's self-promotion is habitual. The habit is deeply entrenched, but Phil is not shameless. Often he catches himself midconversation, shamefully recognizing that he's been going on and on about himself. *Again.* He catches the awkward glances of his conversation partners, notices that others are talking less and less, and *feels* acutely his social free fall as people seize on opportunities to exit the conversation. Sometimes he catches himself in time to make a self-deprecating remark about how he's been going on too long about himself. But the realization often comes too late and there's nothing for it but to drive home from the party with the shameful recollection of his self-promoting ways. Unlike with Janet, there is nothing obviously laudable about Phil's habitual self-promotion. But whatever his other faults, he is not a *shameless* self-promoter. He regularly *feels* the loss of social capital that is his as a consequence of his constant self-promotion.

When Is Shame Appropriate?

Steve is shameless. He feels no shame in connection with his habitual self-promotion. Janet and Phil, though they self-promote, are not shameless. But why *should* Janet and Phil (or Steve, for that matter) feel shame in the context of their own self-promotion? Why is the experience of shame—that painful recognition of diminished social significance—apt for these conversational situations?

To answer that question, consider the difference between promoting yourself and being promoted by another. When another person successfully promotes you, your social capital increases. You are elevated and endowed with significance you did not previously enjoy. This is true whether or not you are aware of having been promoted—it is a social fact. We can (and often do) acquire and lose social capital without any awareness that the gains and losses are occurring. If you *are* aware that you've been successfully promoted, you will likely *feel* something. You will feel honored. You'll feel the lift associated with being thought a person of greater consequence. But there may also be occasions when you are honored and don't *feel* honored (if only because you are not aware that you're being honored).

Now consider successful *self*-promotion. Here again, to the degree that the promotion is a success, your social capital increases. You are elevated and endowed with a perceived significance that you did not enjoy prior to the promotion. These are social facts that follow in the wake of *successful* promotion (be it promotion by another or self-promotion). But notice that in the case of self-promotion, the elevation (even if real) is diminished by the fact that you yourself have done the promoting. You are not elevated to the heights that you would have been had someone else done the promoting. That it is an act of *self*-promotion has a diminishing effect on the net success of the promotion. To be a self-promoter is to be wrongly situated vis-à-vis the activity of promoting. Promoting is at its best when it is in the service of another and not of yourself. So even when self-promotion works (when it has the net effect of increased social capital), the activity is at least partially self-defeating. Some degree of social discrediting is built into the very nature of self-promotion.

The social decline is even more pronounced when self-promotion fails. In an unsuccessful attempt at self-promotion, the promoter suffers a net *loss* in social capital. In this case, the activity is not *partially* self-defeating. It is wholly self-defeating. The attempt backfires, and the unsuccessful self-promoter is deprived of some degree of significance. Again, this is because the self-promoter is not well situated to do the promoting. So whether or not an act of self-promotion is a success (whether it results in a net increase in social capital), there is a self-defeating mismatch involved in the act of promoting oneself that has a diminishing effect on social capital.

These are social facts, meaning they are true whether or not they are felt to be true. You can lose social capital and significance without any *felt sense* of that loss. Consider, for example, what happens when someone is the victim of gossip of which they are unaware. They suffer a decrease in social standing, but they don't *feel* the decrease. Similarly, you can be wrongly situated in certain circumstances without *feeling* wrongly situated (perhaps for the simple reason that you're not aware that you're in that condition). Think of the sports fan who shows up early to cheer for their home team and mistakenly sits on the visitors' side of the bleachers. That fan is wrongly situated but does not *feel* wrongly situated—that is, until the opposing team's fans begin arriving.

But now consider the person who is wrongly situated or who has suffered loss of social capital and significance *and* is well aware of their condition. Consider the sports fan surrounded by other cheering fans who are wearing the opposing team's colors or a person who is the victim of pernicious gossip and overhears the rumors. Here we would expect the *actual* misfortune to be accompanied by *felt* misfortune. The person who feels nothing in these imagined circumstances suffers an affective blindness. Their emotional life is not tracking with the reality of their situation—it's not attuned to the truth that surrounds them.

Let's return to our earlier examples. We agree that Steve, Janet, and Phil are all self-promoters. But Janet and Phil have fitting affective responses to the decrease in social capital that comes as a consequence of promoting themselves. And they do, with varying degrees of success, deploy strategies (e.g., self-deprecation) to rectify the situation. Steve does not. There are emotions apt for losses of all kinds—including loss of social standing and significance—and Steve does not experience them. He is, in this respect, *affectively misaligned* with his environment.

Or, to put it simply, he is shameless.

A shameless person suffers a form of affective misalignment. They lack the affective response that is appropriate to their circumstances. They are like the person who does not feel a sense of horror when confronted with truly horrific, evil events, or the person who lacks terror in the face of the truly terrifying. They are akin to the person who lacks joy when good fortune befalls someone they love or fails to feel loneliness when deprived of companionship. They are similar to someone who lacks sadness when their close friend and neighbor moves to another country or who lacks feelings of betrayal when they have been betrayed. Just as there are fitting affective responses to horrors, to danger, to a beloved's good fortune, to the loss of proximity to close friends or companionship, and to betrayal, there is a fitting affective response to social discrediting—a condition often occasioned by the fact that *one is somehow wrongly situated in a social context.* That response is shame. And, as we will see, shame's opposite is honor. Honor is what you feel when you are lifted up in society that matters to you. Shame is that opposite emotion—what you feel when you are socially discredited in society that matters to you.

Even with this understanding, defining shame is still tricky. Emotions are, in general, difficult to define. Imagine trying to define sadness for someone who didn't know what it was. What would you say? Likely, you'd point to circumstances that usually lead to sadness and say something like, "It's that negative emotion you experience when your dog dies or your friend moves away." But if someone cannot *see* the similarity in affective responses to the circumstances you provide them—if they cannot identify the common emotion evoked in these situations—you may not be able to help them understand sadness.

Not only emotions are difficult to define. Imagine trying to define the color yellow for someone who had never seen anything yellow or, worse, could not *see* what bananas and lemons have in common even when the fruit is right in front of them. You would be trying to define something for someone who lacks the relevant experiences, even in circumstances that ordinarily give rise to those experiences. You'd likely conclude that they suffer a kind of blindness that precludes full understanding of the nature of the color yellow. This is because the best (and perhaps only) way to define some things is to call attention to them—to *point* to them in experience.

Shame is like that. It is the affective response apt for and characteristic of the experience of social discrediting in society that matters to you. It is often a consequence of being wrongly situated in the world or somehow socially out of step. The easiest way to clarify what shame and shamelessness are for someone else is to consider circumstances fitting for shame and compare folks who have the relevant emotion with folks who don't. We've already seen that self-promotion creates circumstances apt for shame. Here are a few other circumstances where shame seems appropriate.

To be naked in public absent any negative affect associated with the corresponding loss of social standing is to be shameless. We all live within the context of cultural and social agreements with those around us that determine what counts as "appropriately dressed." These agreements may be explicitly stated in the form of laws or dress codes of one kind or another. But more often than not, they are implicit agreements. One is expected simply to know what is and is not appropriate. These agreements vary from setting to setting, and we are (or at least should be) aware of the difference between attire that is in good keeping with these agreements—whether we are relaxing at the beach, shopping at the mall, or attending a funeral service. If you go straight from the beach to the funeral without changing your attire, you will likely suffer a decrease in your social standing. If you don't *feel* that—if you suffer no emotional discomfort wearing nothing more than your swimsuit to the funeral—then your emotions are not well-aligned with your reality. You're shameless.

While these agreements about proper attire vary across cultures and settings within a culture, they nearly always include *some* degree of covering for public spaces. Nakedness is a private affair. So to find yourself in the presence of *public* nakedness (whether or not you are the naked one) is to be wrongly situated with others vis-à-vis nakedness. If you have no emotional response to this, you are not affectively aligned with your environment. You're shameless.

We can generalize this example and apply it to a variety of situations. We have all kinds of agreements with one another, and they vary between people groups and certain contexts within those groups. Violating these agreements carries with it a penalty of social discrediting, and a person who is affectively insensitive to these penalties is shameless. As a college professor, I am especially sensitive to agreements that govern instructional spaces. One such agreement dictates that the amount of time someone spends talking should be in proportion to their relative expertise on the topic as compared with others in the room. In general, the less you know, the less you should say and the more you should listen. In almost every class I teach, at least one student exhibits an affective insensitivity to the social decline that is theirs when they routinely violate this agreement. The student talks too much. And the loss of social capital he experiences is palpable. But he doesn't feel it. He's shameless.

For better or worse, these agreements govern our lives together and they are found everywhere. They tell us how to sit, how to stand, how to eat, how to greet one another, how loudly you should speak, how you should smell, what your body should look like, what your house should look like, how close your body should be to the bodies of those around you, with whom you should associate, and much more. And social capital is constantly acquired, retained, and lost depending on conformity with these agreements. Again, this is all true *whether or not* we are aware of the transactions as they occur.

These agreements are mostly implicit, and our knowledge of them is mostly tacit, meaning these agreements are not clearly stated anywhere and our consciousness of them is rarely articulate. But we know them. Ordinarily, we live most of our days in conformity with these agreements without any special effort. One of the interesting and exciting parts about international travel is experiencing another culture and a different set of agreements. These adventures help us to reflect explicitly and consciously on the agreements that shape various communities around the world.

Nearly every tourist must live through the sense of being a fish out of water—the shock of a different culture with different social norms. This is the experience of nonconformity with the social agreements—the experience of being wrongly situated in a society of respectable others. Decreased social capital generally accompanies this nonconformity since the nonconformist is often a source of inconvenience, discomfort, or even pain for those around them. Those respecting the agreements must somehow come to terms with the tourist. They must instruct, correct, accommodate, or somehow look past the nonconformity to get on with their life together.

At some point in their travels, most tourists suffer a loss of social capital. They make a cultural faux pas or look foolish. But not all tourists are shameless. For most, there is a negative emotional response to their experience of nonconformity. Most feel themselves to be somehow wrongly situated, and they feel the burden associated with being a source of discomfort and inconvenience for the people around them. They feel out of step and they feel, with some embarrassment, the corresponding decrease in their social standing. For most, these feelings motivate a humble learning posture toward indigenous groups. They motivate malleability, pliability, and (importantly) a desire to escape attention—to get out of view.

But not for the shameless tourist.

The shameless tourist experiences none of these feelings. The shameless tourist can see that he is out of step. He knows this, and he recognizes that his presence is the cause of needed accommodation. But he doesn't *feel* it. He feels no pressure to conform, reciprocate the accommodating efforts of his hosts, or hide from view. The shameless tourist seems almost to revel in the public display of nonconformity. It is precisely when he should shrink back, disappear from view, and learn a thing or two that he seems given to the loudest and most public displays. He is shameless.

The conditions that usually lead to shame often arise in the context of nonconformity with implicit or explicit agreements about how to be with one another in community.

Failure to conform to these agreements results in social discrediting. For the person with a healthy sense of shame, that will be a source of emotional discomfort. But for the shameless person, no discomfort accompanies their social discrediting.

Notice, though, that we do not have an equally strong degree of concern for every social agreement.

Not long ago, I was on my way to a wedding, and I discovered that I had left my dress shoes in my office. My options were to attend in a dark gray suit with either bright white tennis shoes or bare feet. When I arrived home and informed my wife of my choice, I immediately knew from the expression on her face that I had made the wrong decision. I attended bare-footed and suffered a mild loss in social standing among the respectable others at the wedding as a result.

Now suppose I had instead attended the wedding in proper attire but had in conversation repeatedly used an offensive word or expression to refer to a disempowered people group. In that case, my social standing would have gone into outright free fall. As much as we care about being properly shod at weddings, we care *far more* about using respectful vocabulary to refer to one another, especially when referring to people who've already suffered a great deal. As a general rule, we tend to care more about conformity with rules widely thought of as governing morality than with rules thought to govern matters of etiquette. So our loss of social capital will be greater when we find ourselves in nonconformity with the rules widely thought to govern morality in our context.

These are just the social facts. They are true whether or not we are aware of them. If you fail to publicly conform to strongly held and widely shared moral convictions in your context, you will be subject to sharp social decline, regardless of your awareness of what others think and feel. If you *are* aware of your sharp social decline but have no affective response whatsoever—if there is no negative emotion associated with this precipitous loss of social capital—then your emotions are not well-aligned with your reality. You're affectively misaligned. You're shameless.

The social discrediting that results from nonconformity with agreements widely thought to govern the moral dimension of life is much sharper than the social decline resulting from failures of etiquette. This is why shame is often felt more acutely in connection with moral failure than it is in connection with failures of etiquette. Shame is the negative affective response to social discrediting. So feelings of shame will be stronger when the social decline is more pronounced. This is why strong feelings of shame often accompany the experience of guilt. Notice, though, that this social decline is largely insensitive to the degree to which you share the moral conviction that unifies the group as a whole. Just as you can suffer social decline from nonconformity with rules of etiquette foreign to your own habits and training, you can endure social decline from nonconformity with rules of morality foreign to your own personal moral convictions. In either case, the person with no negative affective response to this social decline exhibits a kind of affective blindness. Her emotions are not well aligned with what's going on around her. She is shameless.

Until now we've been looking at the shame that results from social decline in the wake of nonconformity with social agreements. This nonconformity may sometimes result from wrongdoing, but often it does not. Public nakedness can be the result of a very bad decision. Or it can result from sheer bad luck. Failures of etiquette can be the result of a stubborn and nasty refusal to be polite. Or they can stem from nonculpable ignorance. Nonconformity with widely shared moral norms can be the result of immorality or a widespread mistake about the dictates of morality. So while shame often accompanies and is often most acutely felt in connection with moral failure, the occasion of its occurrence extends well beyond the boundaries of morality.

Shame Is Contagious

Let's conclude our brief tour of the conditions apt for shame by noticing one more important consideration about these conditions: *they are contagious*. Shame is contagious. Shame is contagious because social decline is contagious.

Imagine for a moment that you have been tasked with facilitating a weekly discussion group for victims of sexual abuse. For months you've been meeting with these brave souls and loving them through the painful experience of sharing their stories in order to find company and community with folks who've walked a similar road. As the details of these painful experiences come to light in the slowly unfolding conversation, the group realizes that several members have been abused by the same person. Then one day, and in a particularly poignant moment, it dawns on you and on everyone else in the group that the perpetrator is your father. How would you feel in that moment? What would you say?

Many of us, I imagine, would have a strong desire to make some sort of apology. Yet if pressed to give a reason for the apology, we might find it difficult to explain this impulse. We wouldn't have the same reaction if the perpetrator were discovered to be someone unrelated or even unknown to us. And the impulse, clearly enough, would not be a consequence of you yourself having done something wrong. Instead, it would be an attempt to grapple with a host of related feelings. You would likely begin to experience yourself as a source of discomfort and pain in the group. You'd feel less respectable in the eyes of this group than you had been just moments before—like you were somehow a person of lesser consequence in the wake of the discovery. And you'd feel yourself somehow wrongly situated in the world with relation to sexual predation—despite that you yourself are not a predator.

This is what I mean when I say shame is *contagious*. When someone is socially discredited for being somehow wrongly situated in the world, others closely associated with that person are discredited too. When I fall into shame, I pull others in my relational and social network down with me. This is one of the deep differences between shame and guilt. My guilt, all by itself, does not make anyone else in my social network guilty. But my shame pulls others in my social network into shame as well.

Perhaps the group would try to reduce your shame by insisting that you have nothing to apologize for. Perhaps they'd remind you that you are not responsible for the behavior of your father and express their gratitude for your loving and healing presence in their lives. Still, they'd likely appreciate that you *felt something* in connection with it being your father who did these things. Were you to have responded to the realization that the predator was your father in the same way you would have responded were it a perfect stranger, they'd likely have been offended. Your social decline would have been incomparably sharper. To be emotionally insensitive to your social decline and misplacement in the world as a consequence of the shame of others is to be affectively misaligned with your environment. So it is fitting that you felt the things that you did upon discovering the predator was your father. Were you not to have felt those things, you'd have been shameless.

Association with Jesus

Because shame and honor (unlike guilt and innocence) are contagious, association with Jesus is, and always has been, a pathway to both. In the community that matters most (i.e., the kingdom of God), association with Jesus has always been a pathway out of shame. Jesus routinely identified with the lowly in ways that lifted them out of their shame. The first thing he did, for example, when he discovered that healing power had gone from him into the woman with a bleeding disorder was to address her as "daughter" (Mark 5:33). With that one word, he condescended to identify himself with someone who had fallen deeply into a condition of contagious shame. He said, in effect, "I'm with her—we're like family, she and I." He allowed not only his healing power but also his honor—his social standing—to flow from him to the woman whose body had already been healed. Jesus constantly associated himself with the sick, the lowly, the unholy, the untouchable. And by that association, these untouchable others were lifted from their shame in the community of those following Jesus.

But association with Jesus has also been a fairly reliable pathway into shame. When Jesus healed the blind man in John 9, both the blind man and his parents had to grapple with the shame that accompanied close association with Jesus. His parents simply couldn't bring themselves to tell the religious elite who it was that had healed their son, for fear of the shame that would result. The formerly blind man, apparently made of sturdier stuff, endured the shame of identification with his healer. When given the opportunity to distance himself from Jesus by calling Jesus a sinner, he refused and, as a consequence, was thrown out. He suffered the shame of exclusion from respectable company because of his unwillingness to disassociate himself from his healer.

In a less glorious moment, Peter fled the shame of association with Jesus in his infamous betrayal. This same Peter had recently drawn a sword in defense of his teacher, initiating a conflict in which he would have been hopelessly outnumbered. He was certainly not risk averse. But in a moment of weakness, he could not endure the shame of association with the now-arrested Jesus and disassociated himself three times.

It is still true that association with Jesus can bring both shame and honor. Whatever your shameful past, if you are thought today to be someone walking closely with Jesus, you will be honored in Christian communities—you'll be thought of as a person with greater significance in those communities to the degree that you are thought to be closely identified with Christ. And in 2 Timothy 2:10, 12, we are assured that the destiny of all God's people is one of unimaginable honor as we reign with Christ over the redeemed created order. But, depending on your community, your close identification with Christ can also be the cause of shame. You may be demeaned, ridiculed, or excluded from certain communities because of your association with Christ. And anyone with emotions attuned to their situation will feel the painful sting of that shame.

Shamelessness Is Rampant

To sum things up, shamelessness is a kind of affective misalignment with our environment. The shameless person fails to feel something that is appropriate to feel in her circumstances. The circumstances apt for shame are many and varied. But we can articulate some commonalities. Shame is apt when we are socially discredited in the eyes of others whose opinions matter to us. It is apt when we are in a position to see that we are somehow wrongly situated in the world in such a way as to cause pain or discomfort in others. And it is apt when we are related in certain ways to others who fall into these circumstances. Folks without the relevant affective response to these conditions are shameless.

And shamelessness is rampant. It shows up in the form of increasing immodesty of dress. In educational contexts, it is represented by the rising number of entitled attitudes that students take to their educational experience and in the form of unembarrassed disrespect for teachers. In politics, it turns up in the increasingly brazen and publicly visible departures from widely shared moral standards. In family life, it emerges in the form of increasingly bold and brazen disrespect for parents and guardians. It shows up in many professions in the form of the increasing acceptance of (and even praise for) self-promotion and self-congratulation. And it shows up in religious life and other social networks in the form of unabashed and narcissistic attention paid to one's self and in the disloyalty reflected in the ease and rapidity with which people disassociate with one another and reidentify in some other social location. One goal of this book is to facilitate an understanding of shame in such a way as to stem the contemporary tide of shamelessness.

More needs saying, of course, to motivate our deprecation of shamelessness. Though *something* is clearly wrong with the people in the stories I've shared in this chapter, maybe their shamelessness is a laudable feature of their condition. Maybe it's a *good* thing to be caring less and less about what others think of us or about whether we are rightly or wrongly situated in the eyes of others—even the others who matter most to us. Maybe valuing shame sensitivity as a culture-shaping phenomenon is a mistake characteristic of Eastern wisdom. The eradication of shame would still leave us, after all, with the powerfully negative emotion of guilt for the shaping and correcting of character and behavior. And maybe guilt is all we need. My hope is that the chapters to come will make clear that the valuation of shame is not an Eastern phenomenon and that it shows up repeatedly in the dominant wisdom traditions of the West as well. I will attempt to explain why guilt cannot possibly do the work traditionally assigned to shame in the shaping of a good society. Though it's no doubt true that some people need to worry less about what other people think, it's also true and has been widely recognized throughout human history that the wholesale eradication of shame would be a disaster for human society.

It's good that we care about our standing in society. It's good that we feel something when we are lifted up in society that matters to us. And it's good that we feel something when we are discredited in society that matters to us. Those feelings are honor and shame, respectively. Only someone in the grip of the most radical and pernicious kind of individualism would have no feelings whatsoever about their standing and sense of connection with those who matter most to them. Felt honor and shame go hand in hand with the valuation of community.

CHAPTER 3

SHAME EVERYWHERE

We've seen that shame is the negative emotional response to the experience of being discredited in company that matters to you. This loss of social significance or social capital is often a consequence of finding yourself somehow wrongly situated in social context or related to someone who is wrongly situated. And it characteristically gives rise to a desire to disappear from view.

It is commonly thought that the valuation of shame is a characteristically Eastern phenomenon while the West has been shaped by guilt-centric wisdom. This chapter explores in more detail the relationship between shame and two closely related emotions: embarrassment and guilt. Once the relationships between these three closely related emotions are clarified, we will survey just enough of the Western philosophical canon to substantiate the claim that, until recently, the dominant Western wisdom traditions have embraced shame as well. Even in the West, shame is everywhere.

Shame and Embarrassment

Shame and embarrassment often accompany each other, so it's easy to confuse them. Since we are looking at how they are similar or different, it's important to distinguish them clearly. Embarrassment is felt discomfort with the attention of real or imagined others. You suffer embarrassment when you trip over your own two feet in a public space. You may even suffer embarrassment if nobody is around to see you. You might imagine how clumsy you *would have looked* were anyone around to see.

Shame is characteristically (perhaps nearly always) accompanied by embarrassment—a felt discomfort with the attention of others. This is why shame usually results in the desire to shrink, hide, or disappear. When you've done something embarrassing (or when something embarrassing has happened to you), your natural impulse is to be free of the discomfort of attention by escaping the gaze of others.

It's tempting to say (and some have said) that shame is simply an especially intense feeling of embarrassment. We clearly experience embarrassment to differing degrees. And so it might seem as though shame is just an experience of embarrassment beyond a certain threshold of intensity. Perhaps the cases I've described in the previous chapters as mild instances of shame (being discovered in the wrong moment on a backpacking trip, being in violation of a certain rule of etiquette while traveling abroad, and so on) are better described as embarrassment. Some might argue that we don't experience shame until our embarrassment is of such intensity as to make us feel quite uncomfortable— painfully uncomfortable—with the attention of others.

But this way of thinking about the relationship between

embarrassment and shame overlooks what is most central to shame. It's true that embarrassment can have varying degrees. We all know the difference between a mild feeling of embarrassment (when, for example, we trip over ourselves in a public space) and a mortifying one. Most of us feel a little embarrassed when a friend is effusively and publicly complimentary of us, say, at a party. Imagine, though, being whisked off the street by the Secret Service while on vacation in Washington, DC, ushered into the Capitol building and onto the stage during the president's State of the Union address, and promoted there by the president before the Congress and the millions of people watching on TV as an example of virtuous citizenship because of some of the things you've done in your neighborhood. Most of us would be quite embarrassed indeed. We might even say, in retrospect, that the ordeal humbled us. But we'd not feel shame.

Shame is not simply an intense degree of embarrassment. Shame is the painful feeling of being *discredited* in the company of real or imagined others who matter to you. Shame may or may not accompany embarrassment, yet embarrassment characteristically accompanies shame. But the experience of shame we have when we are embarrassed has nothing to do with the intensity of the discomfort. Shame, like embarrassment, can be relatively mild or unbearably intense. The shame we feel has everything to do with the sense that we've been socially diminished in our perceived weight, worth, or consequence.

Shame and Guilt

Shame and guilt are even harder to distinguish in lived experience than shame and embarrassment since shame and guilt are both negative, self-directed, and unpleasant emotions. The most straightforward way to distinguish them is with reference to their object or target. Guilt takes aim at behavior, while shame aims at the self.

When I feel guilty, my feeling is directed at something I've *done*. When I feel shame, my feeling is directed at my *self*. The difference is sometimes put this way: Guilt says, "I have done something wrong. There is something wrong with what I have *done*." Shame says, "*I* am somehow wrong. There is something wrong with *me*." The easiest way to make clear that these are, in fact, distinct emotional experiences is to imagine situations where someone feels guilt but no shame and ones where someone feels shame but no guilt.

The latter (shame but no guilt) is easier to imagine. For better or worse, people often feel shame when they know they've done nothing wrong. If everyone *thinks* I've done something wrong (even though I haven't), I will likely experience shame. I'll *feel* myself to be a person of diminished consequence in the eyes of respectable others even though I won't feel at all guilty since I know I've done nothing wrong.

In fact, shame is often felt even in circumstances where *everyone* agrees that the one suffering shame has done nothing wrong. Victims of abuse and discrimination often *feel* shame in connection with their victimhood. They feel that the awareness of their victimhood by others (real or imagined) renders them people of lesser consequence. People with publicly discernible impairments or disabilities often feel shame in connection with their disability. Folks in these circumstances feel themselves to be somehow wrongly situated in the world. They feel their own existence as a source of discomfort, inconvenience, and even pain for themselves and for those around them. They feel themselves to be somehow less respected and socially discredited as a result of their disability or victimhood, even though they feel no guilt whatsoever about their condition or their history. Finally, people often feel shame because of what someone else has done or experienced. If my son is arrested for a crime, I'll likely feel shame as a result. But I may not feel guilty for what he's done, especially if I'm convinced that my flawed parenting did not contribute to his misguided behavior. Clearly, then, shame is often experienced in the absence of guilt. That's quite enough to demonstrate that "shame" and "guilt" are not two names for the same emotional experience.

Perhaps less obviously, though, it's possible to experience guilt in the absence of shame. You may feel just a slight pinch of guilt when you exceed the speed limit by more than a little bit and for no good reason. "After all," you might think, "I ought to obey the laws of the land unless there is some good reason to violate them. And there's no good reason for me to be speeding just now." But even if you feel mildly guilty about speeding, you'll likely not feel any shame about it. You'll (rightly) discern that your speeding would not result in any significant amount of social discrediting, even if it were widely known by others.

Or consider the shameless philanderer, someone who is a real womanizer. Perhaps he feels guilty for his most recent bout of flirtation. He can sense that he crossed a line, and he feels guilty for having hurt another person. He is even making plans for his apology. But he is blind to the fact that this recent occurrence is not unusual for him—it is his routine and predictable behavior, the fruit of the person he has become. It is what everyone expects from him, and he is a person of lesser consequence in society as a result. He *does* feel guilty about what he's just done. But he *should* also be ashamed of himself. Yet he is not. He has, in fact, been discredited in company that matters to him because of the person he has become. But he feels no pain from his diminished standing in respectable company. There is no negative emotion directed at his *self*—such as it is. The only negative emotion he experiences is directed at what he has *done*. Shameless people are capable of experiencing guilt, apologizing to others, and requesting forgiveness. Their sincere apologies for what they have done, though, sound hollow and rarely contribute to substantial healing. That's because in their shamelessness, they fail to recognize that it is their self—their character—that needs amending, and not just their most recent behavior.

I hope it is becoming clear that shame and guilt are two distinct emotions. The conditions apt for shame and guilt overlap significantly, which is why they are often experienced together. But they are not the same thing. On the other hand, there are important structural similarities between the two. An examination of these similarities will aid in our understanding of shame and in the attempt to locate where shame fits in a picture of healthy human psychology.

The first thing to notice is that there is an *objective* side and a *subjective* side to both shame and guilt. In both cases, the objective side refers to the conditions that warrant the relevant emotion. The subjective side refers to the emotion itself.

Consider guilt. You can be guilty of an offense because you have done something wrong or illegal (objective side) even when you don't *feel* guilty (subjective side). Perhaps you don't know you've transgressed in the way that you have. Or perhaps you know exactly what you've done and it is a real transgression. But if you don't view what you've done as a transgression, then though you *are* guilty, you won't *feel* guilty. On the other hand, you can *feel* guilty (subjective side) even when you are not, in fact, guilty (objective side) of any transgression. Perhaps you think you've done something that you've not done (you may have a false memory of you doing something you didn't, in fact, do). Or perhaps you know exactly what you've done and you feel terribly guilty about it because you view it as a serious transgression when it's not. Your mistaken belief that what you've done is wrong has you feeling guilty even though you've done nothing wrong.

Our feelings and experience of shame follow a similar pattern. You can undergo shame even when you don't *feel* shame. That is, you can undergo social discrediting—suffering a decrease in your standing, worth, or significance in the perception of others—without feeling the emotion of shame. This most often occurs when you are not positioned to be aware of the relevant social facts. Moreover, you can *feel* shame even when you are perfectly well situated in the company of others and have not been socially discredited in any way. This most often happens when you mistakenly *think* your condition is such as to result in diminished social consequence (or would have that result were it discovered).

It is this distinction between the objective facts and the feelings of guilt and shame that generates the possibility of affective misalignment. When all is going well, feelings of guilt and shame are fitting for the realities that occasion them. Sadly, however, feelings of guilt and shame often arise in such a way as to be misaligned with those realities. The previous chapter explored in detail one particular kind of misalignment—shamelessness. We call someone shameless who does not *feel* shame in the conditions apt for feeling shame. Similarly, we accuse someone of being "without a conscience" if they do not *feel* guilt when they are, in fact, guilty and perfectly well situated to be cognizant of their guilt. The person without a conscience does not feel what a healthy, well-functioning person would feel in their circumstances.

Being without a conscience and being shameless, then, are two ways to be affectively out of alignment with your environment. But they do not exhaust the possibilities. There is the opposite possibility of routinely feeling guilty when you're not guilty. Or you can consistently feel shame when you are not at all wrongly situated in social context—when your condition (even if discovered) would not result in social discrediting. Folks on this end of the continuum are best described as suffering from *chronic* guilt or *chronic* shame, respectively. They feel guilt or shame unceasingly—all the time—whether or not their circumstances befit those feelings.

And there are still additional ways in which felt shame and felt guilt can fail to align with reality. There is the possibility of *feeling* the emotion that befits your circumstances but feeling it with the wrong level of strength or intensity. Shame and guilt, like all emotions, have differing degrees. You can probably tell the difference between feeling a pinch of mild guilt and feeling the gut-wrenching guilt that makes it difficult to focus on anything else. If all is otherwise well, you'll feel the former when you commit a mild error or wrongdoing and the latter only in cases of extreme transgression. But things don't always go as they ought, and so sometimes we feel *really* guilty about the mildest of transgressions. Or we might feel a pinch of mild guilt over some egregious and ridiculously harmful bit of wrongdoing. In these cases, we have the right emotions. But the strength of those emotions does not befit the circumstances.

Felt shame also comes with differing degrees. It can be quite mild or it can be experienced with an intensity that drowns out nearly everything else. If all is going well for you, you'll feel mild shame when you are wrongly situated or socially out of step in such a way as to suffer only modest social discrediting. Perhaps you've just realized that you have transgressed some bit of etiquette while being hosted in a foreign country—eating when you should not have or saying the wrong thing at the wrong time, for example. The degree to which you feel shame will be more intense in accordance with your descent into social discrediting. Consider, for example, how you might feel being publicly accused of a serious moral offense by a credible witness. But, of course, things do not always go as they ought. Sometimes we feel intense shame, though our social standing has suffered only a minor blow. Or we experience mild shame when our social credit is in free fall. In either case, the strength of the emotion does not befit the circumstances.

Finally, both shame and guilt can be experienced with a *duration* unbefitting the circumstances that call them forth. You may experience guilt where guilt is warranted and with the degree of intensity befitting your offense. But you may *continue* to experience the guilt long past the time when, in a healthy psychology, the feeling would have faded or disappeared. You've processed the wrongdoing adequately. You've apologized. You've received a word of forgiveness from the person you've wronged. But the guilt persists. We sometimes say of such people that they "can't forgive themselves." Or you may experience guilt where it is warranted and with the degree of intensity befitting your offense. But the feeling may be too short-lived. If you apologize *very* quickly after an offense, you may receive a word of forgiveness *in very short order.* But if the offense was serious, there's something not quite right about a flash of intense guilt that lasts only the minute or two it takes for that interaction to occur. The same is true of shame. Like guilt, it can be *too* long-lasting or *too* short-lived, given the circumstances.

So we've seen how shame and guilt are distinct. Each can be felt in the absence of the other. But they are also deeply related to each other. Both are self-reflective, negative emotional attitudes. And they share a similar structure or pattern in how we experience them, so they are capable of misfiring in similar ways. They can be felt when they shouldn't be. They can be absent when they should be felt. They can be felt with the wrong degree of intensity. And they can be felt for the wrong amount of time. These misalignments are true of all human emotion. You can, for example, be sad when there is nothing to be sad about. You can fail to be sad when your circumstances are sad in the extreme. Your sadness can have an intensity unbefitting its occasion. And your sadness can be too long-lasting or too short-lived. The same is true of fear, anger, betrayal, and a multitude of other emotions. A perfectly healthy experience of the emotions would have us feeling emotions that befit our circumstances with a fitting degree of intensity and for an appropriate amount of time.

All human emotion, then—be it shame, guilt, fear, or anger—can find healthy and unhealthy expression. And this short reflection on the many ways emotions can misfire should give us an appreciation and longing for a truly healthy (or even relatively healthy) emotional life. A character shaped in such a way as to bring forth *fitting affective responses* to a wide variety of circumstances is something to admire.

Shame in the West

It goes without saying that cultures shaped by the great wisdom traditions of the East (perhaps especially those shaped by Confucianism) identify shame and honor as central concerns. If you spent your formative years in a Confucian-shaped environment, then you know well the contours of the experience of shame we're covering in these chapters. You likely have a trained sensitivity to upward and downward social movement—be it a result of something about you or the result of something about another person to whom you are significantly related. And you know the pressure to conform to the implicit and tacitly-known agreements of your group to avoid the painful experience of shame, both for yourself and for those related to you who would suffer shame were you to fall into sharp social decline.

It does *not* go without saying, however, that until relatively recently the categories of shame and honor have also significantly informed Western culture. You might be even more surprised to hear me suggest that shame and honor *continue* to move Western society, even as the embrace of shame's denigration is gaining widespread approval. It is an ironic feature of contemporary Western culture, most visibly on display in our social media interactions, that we seek to eradicate felt shame as an unhealthy phenomenon even as we wholeheartedly embrace *shaming* as a strategy for curbing bad behavior and fueling social movements. As we'll see in the coming chapters, this is a matter of getting it all exactly backward. We ought to be less suspicious of shame and more suspicious of shaming, since shame can do its work without anyone taking it upon themselves to shame another.

For now, our goal is to draw attention to shame as it has appeared in the dominant streams of wisdom informing Western culture. This will not be an exhaustive survey of shame in Western philosophy. It won't even come close, as that is a project which would require another book altogether. My goal here is to point to shame in a few recognizable Western thinkers to make it clear that shame, far from being a particularly Eastern sensibility, has been an object of concern in the dominant Western philosophical traditions as well.

The dominant Western philosophical wisdom traditions are generally thought to have their origins in ancient Greek thought. So a natural place to begin in our attempt to locate the place of shame in Western philosophical thought is with the ancient Greek poets and philosophers.

In his book *Shame and Necessity*, Bernard Williams argues that the heroes of Greek poetry felt a kind of compulsion—a necessity of action—that could not be reduced to the necessity of determinism or of moral duty. Certain things they felt they *must* do. But they were not compelled by inviolable laws of nature to do them. Nor were they drawn to them by the desire to stay in good keeping with the moral law. Rather, they were compelled to do them because their self-respect could not abide the alternative. The necessity in question, as Williams describes it, says that I must do *this* thing (or refrain from doing it) because *this* is the action that the people I respect would approve. It's the only action I can take that preserves my own self-respect.[1]

This sort of necessity governs many kinds of activities. Examples include avoiding public nakedness or resisting the urge to flee the battlefield. Failures of this sort were causes of shame where the individual would lose respect. First, they would lose the respect of the "respectable others" of society. Often, a loss of self-respect would follow on the heels of that first loss. There are other examples as well in Greek poetry and literature, including situations that *must* be avoided at all costs:

- being a common man and speaking in the assembly
- being a god and getting too friendly with a mortal
- cheating in warfare
- sending your mother away to fend for herself
- appearing before your spouse in rags[2]

The point in mentioning these is not to decide whether these behaviors warrant shame. Our cultural norms and values will inevitably differ from those of the ancient Greeks. The point, rather, is to see that for the Greeks, shame was vitally important as a means of curbing undesirable activities and behaviors that were within a person's power to do and were not, at least in any obvious sense, in violation of a moral rule. Shame was the emotion that motivated the preservation of self-respect. For the Greeks, there were some things that *respectable* people simply did or did not do. And it was the avoidance of shame that kept folks in line.

Unsurprisingly, the Greek philosophers developed this emphasis on shame in their characterizations of virtue and the good life. In Plato's *Euthyphro*, shame is the fear of having a bad reputation. Aristotle's *Rhetoric* adds that it is a bad reputation *among those one respects* that generates the painful experience of shame.[3] In fact, shame can be the result of public *admiration* from the wrong kind of people. And being *negatively* viewed by disrespectable folks can be a cause of honor rather than shame. Getting yourself hated can give you an upward bump in social standing so long as you're hated by folks that are, themselves, hated by respectable others.

For Aristotle, the virtues of a good person are to be found in the golden mean—the conceptual space between two opposite vices. Courage, for example, is located between rashness (being too quick to confront danger) and cowardice (being too slow to confront danger).[4] Generosity is located between prodigality (giving too much) and being stingy (giving too little).[5]

Similarly, one can have too much or too little shame. For Aristotle, modesty is that trait of excellent character that falls between bashfulness (too much shame) and shamelessness (too little shame). The bashful take alarm at everything, while the shameless are abashed at nothing. Modesty is the golden mean.[6]

Shame is important for the Greeks since it is one of the most effective resources for resisting temptation. As Jessica Moss nicely explains, it is an ally of reason in the attempt to reign in the appetites of the soul. Shame makes it clear that, deep down, we care about belonging to our group. And this concern that we have to belong can sometimes keep us in check even when our reason has been coopted by rationalizations.[7]

Jumping ahead in our brief survey of shame, from the ancient to the medieval world, we consider the influence of Thomas Aquinas. For Aquinas, shame is part of the virtue of temperance.[8] Though shame is a profoundly uncomfortable emotion, cultivating a sense of shame is an aspect of properly caring for yourself by preserving your sensitivity to anything that devalues you as a person.[9] For Aquinas, the love of moral excellence, especially the relational aspects of moral excellence, will naturally give rise to a negative emotional response to anything that puts one in a position of shame. Interestingly, Aquinas does not think that a *perfectly* virtuous person will experience shame. So the tendency to feel shame, strictly speaking, cannot be considered a virtue. But his reasons for thinking this are important to understand. For Aquinas, the perfectly virtuous person will successfully avoid *both* evil *and*, importantly, all appearance of evil. So he will not be in danger of the reproach of respectable others. Put a bit differently, the perfectly virtuous person will not feel shame, because they will successfully avoid any and all circumstances that befit shame.

Since, according to Aquinas, shame is not an emotion that the perfectly virtuous person feels, it's tempting to think that Aquinas would have supported the elimination of shame on the path to virtue. But that interpretation misunderstands what he's saying. While it is true that the absence of shame, for Aquinas, is a consequence of having achieved perfect virtue, for those of us who have not yet achieved a state of perfect virtue, there is a derivative sense in which the proneness to shame *is* a virtue since it moves us in the direction of temperance and the moderation of our appetites. So while the perfectly virtuous person would feel no shame, for most of us shame is a fitting and fruitful emotion. Shame aids us by giving us the motivation we need to avoid any appearance of evil.

In this respect shame is similar to guilt. The perfectly virtuous person will find no occasion for feeling guilty, and the tendency to feel guilt is not a virtue. But we would not try to help someone into virtue by trying to prevent them from feeling guilty. The feeling of guilt is a necessary step on the healthy path toward virtue. And progress along this path has, as a natural byproduct, less and less experienced guilt. Aquinas sees shame the same way.

Jumping ahead another several centuries, the seventeenth- and eighteenth-century British empiricists are widely recognized for shaping the dominant moral attitudes in Western thought, even up to the present day. We should certainly add their voices to our historical survey of shame. John Locke, for example, warned parents against the attempt to correct their children with the mere *physical* pain of a beating. When parents exercise corporal punishment, they ought to do it in such a way that the "smart of it" is not the primary punishment since the memory of that experience fades quickly.[10] The shame of the whipping, on the other hand, will stick more effectively in the child's memory.

For David Hume, shame is the opposite of pride. Shame is a simple and negative experience of the self (as distinguished from behaviors of the self). It is the fear of this painful experience of the self, thought Hume, that motivates us to be honest even when we can get away with a lie. It is not simply the fear of feeling guilty for lying but also the fear of shame—the fear of experiencing *oneself* as a liar that motivates truth-telling.[11]

For Hume, shame also plays an important role in punishment and law enforcement. Punishment should not simply be a matter of retribution—not simply a matter of exacting justice on the wrongdoer. Punishment should also be aimed at reforming the criminal. The fear of shame, thought Hume, more powerfully motivates the criminal to reform their character than could the fear of guilt alone.[12]

At this point, you may be wondering, Should we, today, endorse some of these views about shame's role in private and public affairs? I think you're right to ask this question. For my part, I think there is much to disagree with in the treatment of shame in the so-called Western philosophical canon. The point of this short historical survey is not to advocate for a return to any particular view of how shame should operate in public and private affairs. I'll have more to say about legitimate (and illegitimate) expressions of shame in later chapters. The point of this historical survey is simply to demonstrate that shame has a long history in the Western tradition. It is not a particularly Eastern idea that shame should play a central role in our pursuit of the good life. Shame is everywhere—in both the East and the West—and has always played a crucial role in character development.

That said, as we look at the past two centuries of Western philosophy, finding recognition of the positive contribution of shame to public and private life is far more difficult. Contemporary emphasis has been on the individual, on autonomy, and on authenticity, and this has made it more difficult for shame to be viewed as a helpful or fruitful emotion to cultivate.

Shame is, after all, an inherently *social* emotion. It is the painful experience of yourself *as viewed by respected others*. So it finds its place more naturally in conceptions of the good life that emphasize the relational dynamics of human existence. Shame becomes irrelevant to the degree that the self can be defined and evaluated *without* any reference to others. And it is positively at odds with human flourishing to the degree that the good life is understood in largely individual terms—as the authentic expression of one's personal nature without any reference to the norms and agreements of others.

This movement *away from* the relevance and value of shame, though, is a relatively recent and isolated phenomenon in the larger context of human history. Though there are divergent views about how shame should function in public and private affairs, the dominant wisdom traditions around the globe have spoken with something approximating unanimity throughout human history of the importance of the negative self-reflective feeling of shame. The denigration of shame as an inherently destructive emotion that is all too common today is unique to our contemporary Western context. Insofar as we embrace the denigration of shame, we depart from the global, historical, cross-cultural consensus of humanity's wisest voices. These departures are sometimes warranted. But a humble approach will reject this kind of global historical consensus with a fair bit of trepidation.

CHAPTER 4

THE CASE AGAINST SHAME

I've argued that the recent denigration of shame in contemporary Western thought is a departure from the historical global consensus in both the East and West. But I've also noted that such departures are sometimes the result of genuine *progress* in our thinking about human flourishing. Even if the global consensus throughout human history has been xenophobic, tribalistic, and accepting of slavery and misogynistic gendered hierarchies, a society (be it Eastern, Western, or otherwise) makes genuine progress insofar as it finds its way free of the global, historical human consensus along these lines. Since the elimination of slavery, gendered hierarchies, tribalism, and the like is conducive to human flourishing, we should say good riddance to those tendencies, whether or not they have been widely accepted throughout human history. Similarly, if the eradication of felt shame would contribute to human flourishing, we should say good riddance to it as well.

As it turns out, there is a growing body of empirical research in the social sciences suggesting that this is precisely our situation. Recent research suggests that shame, unlike guilt, is an inherently toxic human emotion. While guilt is uncomfortable and painful, it has the potential to move us in directions that are healthy and good for us. It moves us to self-correction, to the righting of wrongs, to reparations for harms done, and to other positive, moral actions. Shame, we are told, is inherently dysfunctional, destructive, and lamentable. It seems we would do well to find our way free of felt shame altogether.

According to this growing body of empirical psychological research, there is a demonstrable correlation between feeling shame and things we know to be destructive, like anxiety, depression, eating disorders, suicide, aggression, rage, and violence. The uncomfortable self-directed feeling of guilt, on the other hand, does not seem to correlate with these lamentable tendencies. So if guilt can do everything we want an unpleasant moral emotion to do—without the toxic self-destructive effects of shame—then why not bid farewell to shame and leverage guilt in seeking moral correction? This is the counsel of a growing chorus of influential voices, recommending that we find our way free of guilt's toxic evil twin, shame.

At the time of this writing, Brené Brown's TED Talk on shame and vulnerability has over fifty-two million views.[1] Brown and others, drawing on the research of social scientists such as June Tangney, are shining a bright light on the profoundly destructive potential of shame to disrupt human flourishing. There has been an explosion of books and resources aimed at helping people find their way free of this ugly and harmful emotion. Though the many who have spoken out against shame do not speak with a single voice about shame's destructive capabilities, they agree with Carl Jung's assessment that shame is a soul-eating emotion.

Brené Brown describes shame as the most powerful master emotion, one that leaves us living in fear that we don't measure up and that we're incapable of change. Curt Thompson characterizes shame as the neurobiological effect of evil's assault on God's good creation. It is one of the two dominant affective forces (the other being love) that represent the cosmic struggle between good and evil. Whereas love tells the Holy Spirit's story of God's embrace and acceptance, shame tells the shame attendant's counternarrative of inadequacy and brings trouble wherever it goes. Christine Caine sees shame as a toxic waste that leaks from wounds and wounded people. Jesus, she says, came to shame our shame. Alan Downs points out how shame disrupts our ability to self-validate. It keeps us from knowing that what we think, feel, and dream is acceptable and legitimate, no matter what other people think and say. And the title of Nadia Bolz-Weber's recent book, seemingly meant to communicate not a shortcoming but an ideal or virtue, is *Shameless*. (As an aside, I was thinking of using that title for *this* book before Bolz-Weber beat me to it. But as a title for this book, it would have called attention to shamelessness being lamentable.) The details and the nuances describing shame and its effects vary between accounts, but the basic message is loud and clear: Shame is not good for us, and we would be far better off as individuals and in our communities if we were free of it.

If I'm correct in my claim that this message represents a departure from the global historical consensus, then what explains the recent and widespread confidence that shame is entirely and inherently bad for us? How have so many in our cultural context become so firmly convinced that the great wisdom traditions of the past were wrong about shame?

In a word: *science.*

Over the past few decades, the resources of empirical social science have been brought powerfully to bear on the study of human emotion. Social scientists have made impressive progress toward a deeper understanding of the emotions and the role they play in healthy human functioning. The past few decades have seen a variety of empirical studies of guilt and shame that have deepened our understanding of these powerful negative emotions. The most influential of these studies and the literature that surrounds them support what I will call the "asymmetry thesis."

The Asymmetry Thesis

Stated simply, the asymmetry thesis begins with the recognition that shame and guilt are two powerful negative self-directed emotions. Guilt, though uncomfortable and undesirable, plays an important role in well-functioning individuals and societies. Shame, on the other hand, is not only uncomfortable and undesirable but also maladaptive. It detracts from human flourishing. So insofar as powerful negative self-directed emotions sometimes aid healthy human functioning, guilt is viewed as the healthy one and shame as its toxic twin.

It would be an oversimplification to say that our culture's confident departure from traditional attitudes about shame owes entirely to the influence of these recent studies. But empirical support for the asymmetry thesis certainly fuels the ongoing denigration of shame for many, including most of the authors mentioned above. Any defense of shame must come to grips with the empirical support enjoyed by the asymmetry thesis. If shame makes an important contribution to human flourishing, then why do the most well-known empirical studies correlate shame (but not guilt) so strongly with deplorable realities like anxiety, depression, eating disorders, suicide, rage, and violence? What else should we learn from these studies, if not that we should do what we can to find our way free of this harmful emotion?

Answering these questions requires a closer look. How do these studies work exactly? And how have they been used to support the asymmetry thesis? In the broadest sense, empirical support for the asymmetry thesis is a two-step process. The first step is to develop reliable measures of shame-proneness and guilt-proneness. After all, if we're going to show that shame, unlike guilt, correlates strongly with various well-known dimensions of psychopathology (anxiety, rage, and so on), then we'll need a way of locating shame-prone individuals and distinguishing them from guilt-prone individuals. Step two is simply a matter of comparing these two populations for well-established indicators of the relevant pathologies.

For our purposes here, it is step one that is most crucial. To confidently correlate shame-proneness with pathologies of various sorts, you want to be sure that your measure is reliably tracking felt shame. If there's any reason to suspect that the measure you use is tracking anything *other* than the tendency to feel shame, then you'll have less confidence that what you're correlating with pathology is, in fact, shame. So what kind of measure might one use to isolate shame-prone individuals? How can we figure out whether people tend to have guilt *or* shame related feelings?

Here's an intuitive idea: ask them. Offer people a list of adjectives associated with guilt (e.g., remorse, regret, deserving of criticism) and shame (e.g., feeling ridiculous, feeling humiliated, feeling stupid) and ask them how frequently they have the related feelings. This "adjective checklist" approach is used by several studies of guilt and shame. The examples given are taken from one popular and well-established adjective-checklist study called the Personal Feelings Questionnaire (PFQ). Participants in these studies are simply presented with a list of adjectives and an opportunity to report on the frequency with which they have the relevant experiences. Subjects are considered shame-prone to the degree that they indicate a high frequency of shame-related emotions and guilt-prone to the degree that they indicate a high frequency of guilt-related emotions.

The beauty of studies like the PFQ is their directness. We measure shame-proneness and guilt-proneness by simply asking people how frequently they have the relevant experiences. But these studies are not without their drawbacks. Chief among them is their reliance on participants' mastery of a fairly subtle emotional vocabulary. These surveys yield useful data only to the degree that participants can reliably distinguish between the concepts of guilt, shame, remorse, and regret, among other emotions. This may limit the reliable data gathered to the relatively highly educated participants. And it presents challenges when translating the study for non-English-speaking participants.

For these and other reasons, social scientists have developed less direct, scenario-based measures of guilt- and shame-proneness. In these studies, participants are presented with a short description of a scenario and are asked to report on the likelihood that they would respond to the imagined scenario in a few ways. Some of the responses are taken to indicate felt shame, while others are taken to indicate felt guilt. For example, a subject is invited to imagine being out with a group of friends when they find themselves making fun of a friend who isn't there. Subjects are then asked whether the following three responses would match their own, on a scale from "not likely" to "very likely": (a) You would feel small . . . like a rat. (b) You would think that perhaps that friend should have been there to defend himself/herself. (c) You would apologize and talk about that person's good points.

Subjects are considered shame-prone to the degree that they select shame-coded responses to the imagined scenarios (option (a) in this example) and guilt-prone to the degree that they select guilt-coded responses (option (c) in this example).

This specific example is taken from a measure called the Test of Self-Conscious Affect (TOSCA). The TOSCA is (and has been for some time) the most well-known and widely used measure of guilt- and shame-proneness. Its popularity owes, in large part, to the ease with which it can be adapted to a variety of situations. Unlike adjective-checklist measures, it does not require mastery of a nuanced emotional vocabulary. It demands only the ability to imagine the relevant scenario and to recognize the emotional, cognitive, or behavioral contours of the envisioned responses. For this reason, the TOSCA has been translated into several languages and adapted for use with a wide variety of populations (including children, adolescents, college students, adults, and prison inmates) to the point where it has now generated an enormous body of data measuring shame- and guilt-proneness. It is not an overstatement to say that the TOSCA has shaped perspectives on guilt and shame for the past thirty years—*more than any other empirical study*. And relevant to our current discussion, TOSCA consistently supports the asymmetry thesis. According to

TOSCA results, shame (unlike guilt) is a reliable predictor of psychopathology.

It is interesting to note that other measures of guilt- and shame-proneness have *not* reliably supported the asymmetry thesis. Subjects who score high for PFQ-measured shame, for example, are no more prone to the relevant pathologies than are subjects who score high for PFQ-measured guilt. A high PFQ score for *either* of these negative self-directed emotions predicts pathology. PFQ data support the thesis that *either* of these emotions (guilt or shame), if extreme, unregulated, or otherwise out of balance, will detract from flourishing. Consequently, PFQ data, unlike TOSCA data, are perfectly consistent with the global historical consensus that *both* of these emotions, if balanced and healthy, have important work to do in well-functioning individuals and communities.

But why this difference in results? Why do TOSCA results so reliably support the asymmetry thesis, while PFQ results don't? And which studies should we trust? The fair thing to say, I think, is that the science is still under construction. Social scientists are, as you might imagine, busy about the work of improving these measures so as to achieve consensus and corroborating support for the various theses they are exploring. So, on the one hand, we should wait and see as further research is done. On the other hand, if you're looking for reasons to be suspicious of TOSCA, reasons to take its support for the asymmetry thesis with a large grain of salt, they're not hard to find.

First, many (if not all) of the TOSCA scenarios represent occasions where responses coded for guilt-proneness are intuitively (and quite obviously) appropriate and balanced. Scenarios include occasions when you've done something wrong, made a mistake, accidentally broken something, or caused harm of some kind. The responses indicative of guilt-proneness include the felt need to apologize, make reparation, take responsibility, or do things differently in the future. Since the constructive and interpersonal responses taken by TOSCA that indicate guilt-proneness are ones that most of us would deem appropriate and healthy, it should not surprise us that a high TOSCA guilt-proneness score fails to predict pathology. The survey consistently presents guilt as a more balanced and healthy emotional response.

On the other hand, many of the responses taken by TOSCA to indicate shame-proneness are intuitively (and quite obviously) imbalanced and extreme. They include:

- thinking about quitting your job when you've broken something at work
- comparing yourself to a rat when you've made fun of a friend
- thinking that you're an incompetent person when the dog you're watching for a friend runs away

These are just a few examples, but they represent the problem with how shame responses are presented. Since most people would intuitively judge these responses to be rank and unhealthy *overreactions* to the imagined scenarios, we should not be surprised to learn that TOSCA shame-proneness predicts psychological unhealthiness.

A related reason to be suspicious of the TOSCA support for the asymmetry thesis has to do with the way shame-indicating responses are framed. Many of them are crafted in such a way that they could just as easily be indicators of low self-esteem or low self-evaluation rather than the tendency to have the particular affective experience of shame. Many of the responses include a self-directed *thought* rather than a feeling or emotion. Examples include:

- *thinking* you're an inconsiderate person
- *thinking* you're a terrible person
- *thinking* you're irresponsible or incompetent

To think of yourself in these terms is to have a low evaluation of yourself—to have low self-esteem. And it was widely known long before the development of the TOSCA that extremely low self-esteem or self-evaluation predicts pathology. So if our attempt to isolate populations prone to shame accidentally gathers up subjects with low self-esteem, it should come as no surprise that this population is psychologically unhealthy.

To sum things up so far, the most direct measures of guilt- and shame-proneness fail to support the asymmetry thesis. They fail to adequately challenge the global historical consensus that shame—no less than guilt—contributes meaningfully to human flourishing when it finds healthy expression. These studies, blind as they are to the distinction between healthy and unhealthy expressions of shame and guilt, measure only the *frequency* with which they are experienced. And they suggest that a high frequency of *either* shame *or* guilt predicts pathology.

But for reasons having to do with their dependence on a developed moral vocabulary, these measures place considerable constraints on the contexts in which data can be collected. Less direct measures remove these constraints, so they are much more widely used and far better known, generating a much larger body of data. These less direct measures, like the TOSCA survey, have informed public discourse on guilt and shame far more significantly than have the direct measures. But as we have seen, these less direct measures seem to be biased in favor of guilt. There's some reason to think that these measures are isolating *only the healthy expressions of guilt* and *only the extreme or imbalanced expressions of shame* (or worse, something other than shame altogether, like low self-esteem or self-loathing). To the degree that the findings of the TOSCA and its surrounding literature motivate contemporary confidence in the departure from global historical consensus concerning the contribution of shame to human flourishing, there's good reason to pause and reflect.

Suppose it's true that the most direct measures of guilt and shame are not in conflict with the historic tradition. What then? What can we say about the psychological effects of shame and shame-proneness? Is it possible there is something *like* the asymmetry thesis that is true and capable of empirical demonstration, even if that particular thesis is false? To answer these questions, we may find some help by shifting from social science to philosophy.

What better place to start than with Aristotle? An Aristotelian perspective on the emotions resists the temptation to divide them into good or healthy ones and bad or toxic ones. It does not, for the most part, ask of a particular emotion whether the healthy person has or does not have that emotion. Rather, it asks *what are the conditions apt for the healthy* expression *of that emotion*. An emotion is expressed in a healthy way when it is the emotion apt in the circumstances that have given rise to it and when it is felt with the proper degree of intensity and for the appropriate amount of time. Unhealthy emotional experiences are those that either (1) do not befit the circumstances that have given rise to them, (2) are felt with a degree of intensity unbefitting in context, or (3) are felt for an unsuitable duration of time.

This is a helpful and nuanced way to think about our emotions, and shame is no exception. Shame is healthy when it is felt in those circumstances apt for its expression and when it is felt with a degree of intensity and for an amount of time appropriate for the context of its occurrence. Otherwise, it is unhealthy (in varying degrees) and (Aristotle might say, if he were in conversation with contemporary empirical psychologists) can be expected to predict all manner of pathology.

Recall what we have learned to this point: that shame is the painful experience of social discrediting. To feel shame is to feel like a person of lesser consequence—to feel one's *self* diminished—in the real or imagined gaze of others who matter to you. It is directed not upon a particular behavior or act but upon one's *self* in social context.

One of the important lessons to be learned from our contemporary attempts to measure shame is that we must be careful not to confuse felt shame with diminished self-esteem. Shame is an affect—an emotional response to one's environment. It is the particular kind of emotional pain naturally experienced upon recognizing that one has been discredited in respectable company. When you have low self-esteem, on the other hand, you *think* or *judge* that you are of little worth, dignity, or ability. To experience diminished self-esteem is to believe you are less worthy, dignified, or able than you previously thought yourself to be. Affectively, low self-esteem feels like self-loathing. Someone with pathologically low self-esteem has, tragically, formed the opinion that they are considerably less worthy, dignified, or able than they truly are. The result is that they routinely experience self-loathing.

Repeated and powerful experiences of shame will likely have a negative bearing on one's self-esteem. Like it or not, we derive much of our sense of self-worth, dignity, and ability from our experience of how others judge or measure us. But insofar as our focus is on shame, we should take care to distinguish it from low self-esteem. It is possible, after all, to experience shame (even quite intense shame) without any corresponding loss of self-esteem. Recall, for example, the shame Jesus Christ suffered on our behalf. Jesus was publicly and falsely accused of something shameful and criminal—claiming to be divine while not divine. As a consequence, he suffered public ridicule and was widely shunned. He was publicly and disgracefully stripped of his clothing, tortured, and killed. To put it mildly, he suffered a precipitous loss of social capital and connection. He was shamed. And according to Christian teaching, if it did not pain him to experience this loss of social capital and connection in company that mattered to him—if he did not undergo felt shame—he was not in all manner of things like us. Presumably, then, Jesus experienced felt shame—intense shame. But just as clearly, he did not suffer a lowering of self-esteem. He did not judge himself to be a person of less worth, dignity, or ability as a result of his experience, and he did not undergo any loathing affect directed at himself. His shame was great, but his sense of his own dignity and self-worth were unassailed.

We might object: "That's Jesus. Can shame be experienced apart from lowered self-esteem for us who are mere mortals?" It certainly can. Imagine being publicly (though mistakenly) accused of an extremely shameful and criminal act. Imagine that the evidence publicly presented, though misleading, is compelling and damning indeed. And imagine that, as a consequence, you are widely shunned and poorly regarded. You would lose social capital and connection and would suffer shame in the communities that matter to you. And if your emotions were tracking the situation in a healthy way, you would *feel* the pain of lost social capital and connection. But your opinion of yourself would not be affected. Knowing you are innocent, you'd not think yourself less worthy, dignified, or able than prior to the accusation. You would suffer intense shame and have the painful emotional experience of your *self* as an object of diminished social consequence in company that mattered to you. You would experience your *self* as a source of discomfort and pain in the world. But you'd not necessarily sink into self-loathing or experience diminished self-esteem—at least not if shame is functioning as it should in your psychology.

To put the point another way, recall that the opposite of shame is *not* dignity, self-worth, or healthy self-esteem. The opposite of shame is honor. Honor, like shame, is a *social* reality. It is a function of how you are connected to and perceived by your social group. And felt honor is your affective experience of those perceptions and judgments. When Jesus was publicly shamed, he suffered a corresponding loss of honor, something he, presumably, both recognized *and* felt. He was dishonored. The author of Hebrews tells us that Jesus despised the shame of crucifixion (Hebrews 12:2). But his dignity and self-worth were unaffected. If shame involves the loss of social capital and connection, honor involves the acquisition of the same. And the author of Hebrews quickly assures us that the shame the crucified

Christ endured and despised was followed by the honor of a seat at the right hand of God.

There are emotions apt for these acquisitions and losses of honor and shame. These emotions will be healthy to the degree that they track the social facts on the ground. Intense and long-lasting felt shame in circumstances of mild social decline (or no social decline at all) is unhealthy. And so is the *absence* of felt shame (or mild felt shame) in circumstances involving extreme social discrediting and the corresponding precipitous loss of social capital and connection.

We're now in a better position to see why many of the empirical measures of shame currently in wide use are not likely to facilitate deep understanding of the psychodynamics of healthy and unhealthy shame. Some of them, it seems, may be tracking something else altogether—low self-esteem, self-loathing, or some mixture of shame, self-loathing, and low self-esteem. Others, while perhaps more reliably tracking shame itself, are not sensitive to the dynamics of healthy and unhealthy shame. They track *frequency* of felt shame. But they do not track the duration and intensity of felt shame. Nor do they tell us anything about whether the felt shame was apt for the circumstances that gave it rise. After all, an emotionally healthy person will *feel* shame quite frequently if, in fact, they are frequently shamed.

For this reason, we should be more hopeful, I think, about scenario-based measures of shame and guilt. Since adjective-checklist studies track mere *frequency* of felt shame and related emotions, they are simply too crude to capture what needs capturing if we're going to observe and distinguish between healthy and unhealthy shame experiences. For a scenario-based study to track the dynamics of healthy and unhealthy shame, though, the scenarios must be fairly nuanced. The various items must depict circumstances involving both mild and precipitous losses of social capital and connection. And the response options must be crafted in such a way as to measure the intensity and duration of the felt shame. A study like this would allow us to determine whether a subject's affective response to social discrediting tends to be fitting for the circumstances that give rise to it. And if we could gather that kind of information about both shame and guilt, we'd be in a better position to determine whether there is an asymmetry in the psychodynamics of these two powerful negative self-directed emotions.

A Modification of the Asymmetry Thesis

As we close this chapter, let's revisit the asymmetry thesis. Recall that at the heart of the thesis is the idea that guilt, though uncomfortable, has important work to do in healthy psychologies and communities, while shame is both uncomfortable *and* toxic insofar as it has been shown to correlate with deplorable realities such as anxiety, depression, suicide, eating disorders, violence, and rage. I've suggested that we should be suspicious of the asymmetry thesis since it cuts against the grain of global historical consensus concerning the role of shame in well-functioning people and societies. And I've argued that there is good reason to temper the confidence frequently derived from the social scientific studies most often cited in support of this departure from global historical consensus.

But is there *anything* true in the asymmetry thesis? Isn't there *something* right about the suggestion that shame is more powerfully destructive, more potentially havoc-wreaking than guilt? It might surprise you to hear me say yes, I believe there is. And in what follows, I'd like to attempt a modification to the asymmetry thesis that will help chart a path forward for an exploration of the positive contribution shame can make in our lives.

Once we're clear that both shame and guilt can be healthy or unhealthy—that both of these emotions can be felt in a way that is fitting (or not) the circumstances that give rise to them—the way is clear to ask more nuanced questions about the relationship between guilt and shame.

We might ask questions, for example, about the *unhealthy* expressions of these two emotions in particular. Do these two emotions pack the same destructive punch when expressed in unhealthy ways? Or does the unhealthy expression of shame have potential to be more damaging? And what about healthy expressions? Does shame (whether healthy or not) contribute more powerfully than guilt to conditions we recognize to be unhealthy, like low self-esteem and self-loathing? If so, then we should evaluate shame and guilt differently even if the asymmetry thesis as currently stated does not accurately capture what should be those differences in evaluation. And once we locate the important differences between the value of shame and guilt, we'll want to be mindful of those differences as we think about how guilt and shame manifest themselves in healthy psychologies and well-functioning societies.

Recall that felt shame is an emotion directed at the *self*. It is the painful experience of your *self* as an object of social discrediting. Felt guilt, on the other hand, is an emotion directed *not* at your self but at something you have done. It is the painful experience of your behavior violating some standard or norm that you care about. It is for this reason that low self-esteem and self-loathing follow much more easily in the wake of felt shame than they do in the wake of felt guilt.

Low self-esteem follows felt guilt because we are profoundly social beings. Our self-concept is (and is designed to be) deeply informed by our experience of how we stand in the eyes of others whose opinions we value. As we've seen, it is perfectly possible to experience shame without suffering any loss of self-esteem. And sometimes it will be predictable that situations should go in just this way (when, for example, you are publicly accused of something you know you didn't do). But because our experience of how others view us so deeply informs our self-concept, experienced decline in social standing will often bring in its wake a diminished appreciation of self-worth. Powerful and repeated experiences of the low view that others take of me will typically result in my having a less firm grip on my own dignity—my own self-worth.

This natural connection between felt shame and the diminished appreciation of self-worth explains the profoundly destructive potential of shame. Felt guilt threatens the pleasant experience of yourself as innocent. Felt shame threatens the much more existentially profound experience of oneself as worthwhile.

For better or worse, most of us are quite good at judging our own behavior negatively while drawing no negative conclusions about our *self* or our character. This "fundamental attribution error" is a well-established habit in human psychology. Psychologists have discovered that when *you* do something wrong, I'll jump fairly quickly to the conclusion that your bad behavior is a consequence of your bad character. But when *I* do something wrong, I'll be less likely to think of my own bad behavior as a manifestation of bad character. I'll be more likely to attribute the error to my circumstances or to an uncharacteristic slipup.

We're very good at protecting the view we have of ourselves against acknowledged bad behavior. I'll let myself off the hook with almost any excuse I can think of. But we're not as good at protecting the view we have of ourselves against the experienced judgments of respected others. When the people I care most about have a low view of me, it's difficult to prevent myself from sliding into agreement with them. *This is why shame leads far more easily to low self-esteem than does guilt.*

I think this explains the temptation to eradicate shame, and it's what drives the chorus of voices we heard earlier in this chapter. We lament (as we should) any occasion on which someone sinks into self-loathing or loses their grip on their self-worth. And since shame so naturally leads to these lamentable conditions, it's tempting to think that the solution is to inoculate those we love against felt shame. The goal—to preserve self-esteem and prevent the slide into self-loathing—is laudable. But the means—the attempt to inoculate people against felt shame—are misguided.

This response is fairly common with negative emotions. We hate to see the people we love experiencing and suffering the effects of painful emotions. So insofar as we can, we want to remove those feelings. When a friend feels lonely, we want to help them out of that feeling, so we bring them companionship. When a friend feels betrayed, we want to help them out of that feeling, so we offer them loyalty and fidelity. When a friend feels shame, we want to help them out of that feeling, so we honor them. This is good and right, as it should be.

But as much as we dislike feeling lonely and betrayed, we might also recognize that it would be a mistake to inoculate someone against these painful emotions—to render them immune to these painful experiences. If a loved one has betrayed you, the emotional feeling of betrayal is fitting. If you do not *feel* betrayed when you have, in fact, been betrayed, then you are affectively broken. Something is wrong. If you find yourself without companionship, loneliness is appropriate. If you do not *feel* lonely when you are without companionship, then you are affectively broken. Something isn't working. What the lonely person needs is not to be inoculated against the painful emotion of loneliness. What they need is companionship. What the victim of betrayal needs is not inoculation against felt betrayal. What they need is loyalty and fidelity. The same goes for shame. If you do not *feel* shame when you have been shamed— when you have, in fact, been discredited and diminished in the eyes of others you care about—then you are affectively broken. Something is wrong. The person who suffers shame doesn't need inoculation against this painful emotion. They need to have their honor restored.

A caveat is in order here because there are occasions when inoculation from pain is *part* of what is needed. If something is pressing your hand against a hot stove, the *deep* need is to address the *cause* of the pain you're experiencing. We need to address and eliminate whatever is keeping your hand pressed against the stove. But you might *also* need to be inoculated against the pain in your hand—extreme as it is. This inoculation project, though, will be focused and temporary. We would not want to render you incapable of feeling pain ever again. That would be a disaster. Pain plays an important role in your flourishing, after all. We would want to render you incapable of feeling pain *in your hand* (perhaps with some ice or aspirin) for a relatively short period of time, a temporary measure on the path to healing and wholeness.

Shame can be extremely painful. When it is, a loving response may very well involve targeted inoculation for the one suffering shame against this particular painful experience. But it would be a mistake to render a person incapable of feeling shame altogether or in any kind of lasting way. Instead, we may want to render them incapable of feeling (or feeling with this level of intensity) the particular shame they are experiencing. When and if we do, we should recognize that we are not addressing the deeper issue. Restoration of honor and inoculation against felt shame are not the same thing. Inoculating someone entirely against felt shame is like making them incapable of feeling pain when they are pressed up against hot stoves. Targeted inoculation is like giving them ice for their burned hand. Restoring someone's honor is like taking away whatever it is that is pressing their hand up against the stove.

Suppose someone is suffering with felt shame, say, because of lost social significance, owing to a publicly discernable impairment or disability. They are thought to be a person of less consequence in communities that matter to them because of their appearance. Suppose their felt shame is extreme—the kind of intense shame that all too often lends itself to self-loathing and tragically low estimations of self-worth. Naturally, we'd want to inoculate them against this particular shame experience. If possible, we'd like to help them into a shame-free experience of their embodied self in the world. That's understandable and laudable.

But it would be a mistake to do this by rendering them

incapable of feeling shame. It would be a mistake for the same reason that it would be a mistake to help someone suffering extreme loneliness by rendering them emotionally insensitive to the loss of companionship. Insofar as folks with physical impairments and disabilities suffer shame in our midst, their *deep* need is not inoculation against felt shame. It is the restoration of their honor. We may need to do some inoculation work in the meantime (just as we would for any extremely painful experience). But the deep work is not the work of eliminating painful shame experience. It is rooting out the causes of pain, which in this case is the social discrediting that comes to people with publicly discernable disabilities. It is deplorable (and, I think, unquestionably true) that folks with publicly discernable disabilities suffer a loss of social capital and connection on account of their appearance. And we do them a disservice insofar as we address that situation by suggesting that the solution is to keep them from feeling the pain of that loss, as though their feeling the pain is the problem.

Even as we attempt to ease their pain, we love them best by honoring them and doing what we can to eradicate those elements of society that have resulted in their loss of social capital. But even as we do this work, we should acknowledge that the painful felt shame they experience is apt for their circumstances. Their felt shame is perhaps the most important indicator of this particular dimension of brokenness in our society. The *last* thing we want to do is to shame their shame. Rather, we should *listen to* and *learn from* their shame. Let their shame be our teacher. We honor those who suffer this kind of shame when we cite their shame as a reason to consider their voices authoritative in conversations about the politics of disability. And we honor them when we allow ourselves to partake in the shame they experience. It is shameful, after all, to be situated comfortably in a society that downgrades folks who have publicly discernable disabilities. We should all be ashamed. We should be ashamed even if we are not among those *guilty* of having brought society into this lamentable condition. And if we were truly ashamed, we might do more to address this aspect of brokenness in our world today.

CHAPTER 5

DEFINITIONAL INTERLUDE

We have seen that the case against felt shame—the argument that shame is a toxic emotion—rests in no small part on conceptual confusion. To see that the contemporary case against shame is misguided, we have to first identify what shame is and precisely distinguish it from other related experiences. So before we move further ahead, let's pause briefly to take stock of the definitions we've articulated. These definitions will assist us in upcoming chapters as we explore more fully shame's contribution to human flourishing.

Guilt: The state one is in after transgressing a standard. There is no such thing as plain and simple guilt. Guilt is always a matter of your relationship to some particular standard. You can be guilty relative to a particular set of laws, relative to the rules of a game you're playing, or relative to the standards of conduct your employer articulated, for example. Moral guilt (in particular) is the state one is in when one

has acted in such a way as to transgress the standards of morality. The opposite of guilt is innocence.

Felt Guilt: The painful emotional experience that naturally accompanies perceived or imagined guilt relative to a standard that matters to you.

You can experience felt guilt even when you are not guilty. And you can fail to experience felt guilt when you are, in fact, guilty. The opposite of felt guilt is felt innocence.

Shame: The state one is in as an object of social discrediting in a community of others.

You undergo shame in some particular community when you have been dishonored or have lost social significance and connection with others in that community—usually as a consequence of being wrongly situated vis-a-vis some widely accepted social norm in that community. The opposite of shame is honor.

Shame always manifests in relation to some particular community. There is no such thing as plain and simple shame—it is always relational. You can undergo shame relative to one community and, at the same time and for the same reason, be subject to honor in another. This will happen when the shared standards in the various communities you belong to differ significantly. When a white prison inmate murders his black cellmate to gain entrance into the Aryan Brotherhood, the Brotherhood will likely honor him for his action. But he'll be subject to shame in the larger community of fellow human beings because of what he's done. The degree to which he *feels* shame or *feels* honor will be a function of the degree to which these two communities matter to him.

Felt Shame: The painful emotional experience that naturally accompanies the perceived or imagined undergoing of shame in a community that matters to you.

This painful emotion is directed at one's self as an object of social discrediting. You can experience felt shame when you have not undergone shame. And you can undergo shame in a community without experiencing felt shame. The opposite of felt shame is felt honor.

Feeling Ashamed of Yourself: The painful emotional experience that naturally accompanies felt shame when you think that the felt shame is deserved.

You'll feel ashamed of yourself when you experience felt shame for the culpable violation of social standards that you yourself endorse. You can experience felt shame even when you're not ashamed of yourself. If I am shamed in a community that matters to me because I've been credibly accused of a shameful crime but I know I'm innocent, I'll feel the sting of that social discrediting. I'll feel shame, but I'll not *be ashamed of myself* since I know I have nothing to be ashamed of.

Embarrassment: Discomfort with the real or imagined attention of others.

You can experience embarrassment whether the attention received from others is loaded with positive or negative evaluation. Embarrassment often accompanies the experience of being shamed, but it may also accompany the experience of being honored. I don't know that there is a precise antonym or opposite for embarrassment. But the unembarrassed person, for better or worse, experiences no discomfort at all with the real or imagined attention of others.

Dignity: The state of having worth or value.

Something or someone with dignity is worthy of respect and honor whether or not it is (or they are) respected or honored. The opposite of dignity is worthlessness.

Self-Respect: The state one is in when one recognizes and appreciates their own dignity.

Notice the two sides of the definition: recognition and appreciation. The recognition is a cognitive act where a person with self-respect accurately assesses her own dignity. The appreciation is affective. A person with self-respect has positive emotional dispositions directed at herself that befit her worth. A person who lacks self-respect will exhibit low self-esteem, self-loathing, or both.

Low Self-Esteem: The persistent and habitual underestimation of one's own dignity.

Low self-esteem is fundamentally a cognitive phenomenon. It concerns thoughts and judgments about one's self. The opposite of low self-esteem is hubris—the persistent and habitual overestimation of one's own ability, worth, significance, or value.

Self-Loathing: The painful emotional experience that naturally accompanies extremely low self-esteem.

Self-loathing is a kind of *felt* hatred, dislike, or disrespect directed at one's self. While self-loathing typically accompanies low self-esteem, the two are distinct. It is possible to have a very low estimation of one's own worth or significance without experiencing any painful felt dislike or hatred for one's self. We don't, after all, feel hatred or even dislike for everything that we take to be of little value. And it is possible for someone to think very highly of their worth, abilities, and significance while also feeling extreme dislike and even hatred for themselves.

Recall that, except in the post-Enlightenment West, there is near perfect consensus among the great human wisdom traditions that felt shame has important work to do in healthy human psychologies and communities. If we are to make any progress in understanding and embracing this near-universal valuation of shame, it will require that we remain clear about these distinctions and differences. We need to grasp, with clarity, these definitions. It will take work and effort *not* to conflate felt shame with embarrassment, low self-esteem, or self-loathing. Vigilance is required since so much of the present-day literature on shame conflates it with these other phenomena. And conflating shame with low self-esteem or self-loathing will all but guarantee that it is toxic—that it has no place in healthy human psychologies.

Since all people possess inestimable dignity, the judgment that one has no (or little) worth, value, or significance (i.e., low self-esteem) is always and everywhere false. And to feel anything like hatred, extreme dislike, or disrespect for oneself (i.e., self-loathing) is to be affectively out of alignment with reality. All people have inherent, immeasurable dignity. Whenever *shame* is used synonymously with *self-loathing* or low *self-esteem* or if it is confused with the absence of self-respect more generally, it inevitably follows that shame, too, will be seen as toxic and harmful.

Some may continue to insist that these terms *are* synonymous in their actual use—that ordinary folks use the words *shame, low self-esteem,* and *self-loathing* synonymously to denote the absence of self-respect. They will argue that our nuance will be lost or perhaps meaningless to most people. How should we respond? I believe that with a little care, most can see that these terms are not synonymous—that they name different phenomena—so that conflating them is wrong and careless. My hope is that the first few chapters of this book have helped you to see that these terms name different (even if interestingly related) experiences.

In any case, we still need *some* word to denote the felt pain of perceived or imagined discrediting in the eyes of others who matter to us. And we need *some* word to denote the good feeling that accompanies perceived or imagined increases in social standing among respectable others. Traditionally (both in the East and West), the words for these experiences have been *shame* and *honor*, respectively. If we abandon these traditional definitions by treating these words as synonyms for words like *self-loathing* and *dignity* and then wish to think together about the role of these undeniable dimensions of human affective experience, we'll need to find new words for these experiences. You can change the definition of a word, but the reality the word describes still exists, and we must call it something.

The problem is that there are no obviously suitable replacements. We could make up a new word like *shlame* to denote what has traditionally been called *shame.* But I fear that would only add to the confusion. It is far better if we proceed with greater nuance and clarity (which is one of the reasons I've written this book), keeping the definitions and distinctions I've outlined in this "definitional" chapter clearly in view.

CHAPTER 6

WHAT SHAME IS FOR

My wife and I long dreamed about taking our entire family on a summer-long RV tour of the United States. We knew that the timing of the trip was crucial. We wanted to wait until our youngest was old enough to appreciate some of what he would experience, but we also wanted to go before our oldest had lost all interest in spending months on the road with his family. It's a tricky balance. The date we settled on was the summer of 2014, and we spent much of 2013 planning and preparing for the trip. We had originally planned to rent an RV for the entire summer. But we quickly discovered that the cost of renting for that length of time was prohibitive. So we settled on buying an older RV we could use for the summer and then selling it when we returned home. We found a twenty-year-old Class C Jamboree Searcher in remarkably good shape with low miles. Jackpot.

Anyone who has owned an older vehicle will know that they develop a personality over time. Each vehicle has its own quirks and idiosyncrasies, and these unique characteristics create a bond between owner and automobile, endearing the automobile to its owner and making it increasingly difficult over time for anyone other than the owner to operate the vehicle. Our Searcher was no exception. Early on the road trip, we quickly discovered one of its more pronounced idiosyncrasies.

About thirty miles into our cross-country trip, a series of loud beeps sounded, alerting us that the driver's seat belt was not engaged. The noise continued for twenty seconds, even though I (the driver) was wearing my seat belt. Then, mercifully, the beeping stopped . . . for thirty minutes. Again, the beeping sounded for another twenty seconds. It soon became clear that the seat belt receptacle was not registering that I was wearing my seatbelt. And the Searcher was designed (sensibly enough) to warn the driver repeatedly (every thirty minutes to be exact) if the driver's seat belt is not engaged.

As you might imagine, I spent much of the downtime during our first couple of stops on the trip trying to solve the problem—with no success. I couldn't get the seat belt receptacle to register the engaged seat belt. And I couldn't figure out how to disable the warning system. So for twelve-thousand miles over the course of three months, the Searcher announced every thirty minutes and for exactly twenty seconds that the driver was not wearing a seat belt. At first it was annoying. Painfully so. Then after enough time passed, we stopped hearing it. Now, five years later (we never did sell the Searcher—too many good memories to let go of it), it's endearing. Whenever we go camping in the Searcher, we're reminded—every thirty minutes—of the glorious summer of 2014, when we saw the country end to end and top to bottom.

Warning Systems

Psychologist and bestselling author Alan Downs tells us that painful emotions are like warning lights—alarms. In this, our painful *emotions* are similar to the physical *pain* we experience. The function of physical pain is to alert us to something happening to our body that requires our attention. Similarly, we are fitted by God, evolution, or both, with painful emotions that alert us to features of our environment that require our attention. The emotional alarm is ringing, and we should take a closer look.

Companionship, for example, is crucial for human flourishing. The painful emotion of felt loneliness alerts us to the absence of companionship and compels us to find union with other people. The painful feeling of betrayal alerts us to the absence of fidelity in our relationships and compels us to seek faithfulness in our current relationships or to seek new relationships where that is a more realistic prospect. Shame, Downs suggests, alerts us to the absence of *validation* and compels us to seek connection and acceptance.[1] This is all perfectly in keeping with our design because we are social beings. We require connection, validation, and faithful companionship to flourish. And it should not surprise us that we are fitted with a set of warning devices (painful emotions) that alerts us to the absence of those requirements.

If you're like me, you have a love/hate relationship with the warning systems in your life. When the light comes on in my car, alerting me that it's time for an oil change, I want nothing more than for it just to go away. Recently, I discovered on YouTube how to disable the check engine light in my Camry, even when I've not proceeded with the necessary services. So experiencing the sweet relief of freedom from that obnoxious red exclamation point on my dashboard is possible! But that's a dangerous "freedom."

Years ago, I drove a Jeep, and like everyone who drives a Jeep, I loved it. At some point, the check oil light in my Jeep went inactive without my knowing it. So the vehicle had no way of alerting me that it was burning oil and was increasingly incapable of doing whatever it is that Jeeps do with engine oil when all is working as it should. It was glorious! I drove for months and months and months without any annoying red lights in my face. There were no warnings. No beeps. No lights. Just the simple joy of driving a Jeep, which only Jeep owners can fully appreciate! That is, until one day when the Jeep suddenly, and without any warning whatsoever, simply stopped running in the middle of my commute from work. It never ran again. That experience has led me to think twice about using the YouTube trick to disable the warning light on my Camry, regardless of how annoying it might be.

Our Searcher RV has an unregulated warning system. This means the connection between the alarm and the reality the alarm is meant to signal has been severed. The warning system is no longer capable of doing what it was designed to do—that is, remind the driver to put on a seat belt. It has become nothing more than a painful annoyance. And, for that reason, it has become something we ignore. But my experience with my Jeep reminds me that warning lights are there for a reason. As sweet as life is without them, we shouldn't want to be free of them altogether.

We all have a complicated relationship with warning systems. Yes, they're annoying. Often painfully so. Sometimes so much so that they are life-disrupting. If you've ever been in a small space where the fire alarm was malfunctioning, you'll know that warning systems can sometimes be loud and painful in such a way as to make it impossible to attend to anything else. The temptation to disable a *dysfunctional* warning system is understandable. But a moment of deeper reflection helps us to see that it's rarely a good idea. The fire alarm is *designed* to make it nearly impossible to attend to anything else. Were there a fire, that's exactly what you'd want—to be incapable of thinking about anything other than escape. When we feel disruptive physical pain, it's understandable that we usually seek to disable the body's system for alerting us to physical harm. We take aspirin—or maybe something stronger. But we know that rendering our bodies forever incapable of feeling pain would be a terrible idea. We all know that pain is there for a reason. And severe pain is *designed* to get our attention.

If you're feeling lonely—deeply and painfully lonely—the thought of a life inoculated against felt loneliness may be attractive. But it'd be a terrible idea to be inoculated against felt loneliness since it is your way of being alerted to the absence of companionship in your life. It's profoundly important, when you are without companionship, to be aware of that fact and to sense the need to seek union with others. If you still felt painfully lonely—even surrounded with meaningful relationships—then it would be understandable if you wished to "disable" your ability to feel lonely. But I hope you can see that this would still be a big mistake. It'd be like disabling your car's oil alert system just because it was malfunctioning. Disabling it is a temporary fix that leaves you vulnerable to future problems. What you need, clearly enough, is a *fix* of the alert system. You need to *regulate* the warning system so that it goes off when (and only when) corrective action is required.

The same is true of shame. If you are a victim of the emotional pain of unregulated, chronic, or persistent shame, then the desire to disable your ability to experience felt shame is perfectly understandable. And just like the YouTube video I found for my Camry, resources abound in recent contemporary literature for disabling your ability to feel shame.

Alan Downs, for example, recommends growing in the ability to self-validate as a strategy for keeping shame's demand for validation and acceptance at bay.[2] As children, we have no alternative but to seek validation from others. We depend on those around us to tell us that we're acceptable—that we're okay. Felt shame is important early in life, since it motivates the acquisition of validation from others that we so badly need as we grow up and develop strong selves. Growth into mature and healthy adulthood, though, brings with it the ability to self-validate. Downs argues that healthy adults no longer have a use for the painful emotion that warns them when they are objects of social discrediting *because they no longer need the validation of others to flourish.* If they've developed strong, stable selves, they are able to provide for themselves all the validation they need. Adults with the healthy ability to self-validate can safely disable the alarm, Downs says. They can safely deploy strategies to silence or eliminate felt shame altogether.

I disagree. The deeper truth is that *you and I are hardwired to need the validation of a group or a community to flourish.* This need is not something we outgrow as we mature into healthy adults. And while it is important to grow in the ability to self-validate (and it is quite important because there can be pathological dependence on others for validation), no degree of self-validation will eliminate our need to be included and accepted in a community that accepts and validates us. The idea that this need can be fully met by me alone is an expression of the radical individualism characteristic of the post-Enlightenment West. It contradicts the nearly unanimous voice of the great wisdom traditions—both East and West—throughout human history. We need each other. And we need to be accepted, included, and validated—not only by ourselves but also by our communities. Our deep need is to *regulate* our emotional experience of shame so that it is properly attuned to the facts. Is it aligned with the reality of our relationship to respectable others? Silencing or disabling our ability to feel shame does us no good.

The Value of Belonging

As we have seen, felt shame is the warning system that alerts us to social discrediting. It is the discomfort we feel with perceived disapproval, disconnection, or discrediting in the eyes of others whose opinions matter to us. Like all warning systems, it can go haywire. Its activation can be disconnected from the realities it is supposed to signal. When the system is dysfunctional, it's painful and disruptive. And it's tempting to disable the warning system—to short-circuit our ability to feel any shame at all. If you're in the spell of post-Enlightenment individualism, captivated by the ideal of complete self-sufficiency, then silencing shame may seem like a good idea. But if community identity and group inclusion are essential to human flourishing, eradicating shame will be a big mistake.

The valuation of shame and of felt shame, then, makes sense only for someone who continues to see the value of belonging. It's for those for whom radical self-sufficiency is *not* the ideal. After all, why would I keep a painful warning system in place to alert me to social discrediting if I don't care about social credit? Radical individualism teaches (wrongly) that human health and flourishing can be had regardless of our inclusion or exclusion in community. Someone enamored of radical self-sufficiency may still have an interest in moral purity. He may want to do what's right and avoid doing what's wrong. So it may make sense to cultivate a warning system that alerts him to his own wrongdoing. Even for the radical individualist, the valuation of guilt will continue to seem sensible. Felt guilt is uncomfortable and painful—even intensely so if we judge what we've done wrong to be heinous indeed. But it functions as an important safeguard against wrongdoing insofar as it makes wrongdoing uncomfortable and painful for us. But if guilt is sufficient to motivate moral behavior, from the standpoint of radical individualism and self-sufficiency, there is no need to add felt shame to the mix. We no longer need felt shame to curb bad behavior since felt guilt is perfectly suited to do exactly that.

The unique value of shame is not found in its ability to provide a check on bad behavior. Guilt can do that. Yet, even though it's not uniquely suited for the task, felt shame can sometimes check bad behavior. When we judge that a certain wrong action tempting us will result in social discrediting, we are motivated by the avoidance of the guilt we'll experience if we succumb, and *also* by the avoidance of shame. But shame is often felt even when there is no question of moral wrongdoing at all.

Recall that shame is experienced when we find ourselves wrongly situated in the presence of, disconnected from, or otherwise socially discredited in the company of others whose opinions matter to us. This can happen *whether or not* we've done anything wrong. It can happen when we violate rules of etiquette. It can happen just because we're related to someone who has fallen into shame. It can happen when we have visible impairments or disabilities. It can happen when we are victims of abuse. It can happen even when we do something that it is right and proper to do. If the people I care about and with whom I wish to share life feel strongly that it is irresponsible or even immoral to give handouts to folks in poverty, I may experience felt shame if I am seen giving aid to a beggar on the side of the road. The primary purpose of shame is *not* to assist guilt in the curbing of bad behavior.

Shame, at its core, is not a check against any particular set of behaviors at all. As we've been learning, the behaviors and conditions that elicit shame in a community will vary from group to group, depending on the shared values in the group. In a healthy community, those values will overlap significantly with moral obligations, but they'll never be exhausted by the rules of morality. There will also be rules of etiquette, for example. And in unhealthy communities, there may be significant dissonance between the demands of morality and the behaviors and conditions that elicit shame. For a morally sensitive person in such a community, felt shame and felt guilt may pull them in opposite directions. I'll feel guilt (the painful recognition of not having done what I ought) if I don't lend a hand to the beggar on the side of the road. But I'll feel shame (the painful experience of myself as an object of social discrediting) if I do.

If shame's unique purpose is not as an additional check on bad behavior, what is it capable of doing that guilt cannot? Shame serves the unique purpose of binding us into communities of mutual interest and investment. This is something that guilt is logically incapable of. I cannot be guilty for anything done by anyone other than me. If my son gets caught selling drugs, I may feel guilty (and may *be* guilty) for not raising him well. But I will not be guilty of drug dealing. At the conceptual level, guilt cannot be applied to anyone other than the person who participated in the illicit behavior. My son's bad behavior may bring to light things of which I *am* guilty (e.g., bad parenting). But I cannot be guilty for what my son has done. Only he can be guilty for that.

Not so with shame. If my son is caught dealing drugs, I am not guilty for what he has done. But I *am* likely to suffer shame. I am likely, that is, to be an object of social discrediting. My standing among respectable others is likely to decrease. If I feel guilty for what my son has done, my feelings are not tracking reality since I am not the one who sold drugs. But if I feel shame because my son's crime is discovered and known, my feelings *are* tracking reality. I am, in that case, an object of social discrediting, and my felt shame is the painful appreciation of that fact.

The Difference between Shame and Guilt

This brings us to the all-important difference between shame and guilt. Shame and its opposite, honor, are *contagious*. Guilt and its opposite, innocence, are not. We talk about "guilt by association." But, in truth, there is no such thing as guilt by association. It may be that your manner of association with the guilty party is a consequence of bad behavior on your part so that you are guilty *for* the association. But you cannot be guilty for something someone else has done *merely* by means of your association with them. Guilt and innocence are inherently individualistic. They accrue to individuals as a consequence of what they (and only they) have done or failed to do. They are, strictly speaking, incommunicable. I cannot become innocent merely by associating with innocent people any more than I can become guilty just by associating with the guilty.

This is true even in contexts where one person represents or somehow stands in for another. If we elect an immoral president who behaves deplorably, we will be rightly judged for having voted that president into office. We'll be guilty of bad electing. And we'll rightly suffer the consequences of having a president who behaves deplorably. Those are our consequences to suffer. But we'll not be guilty of the president's deplorable behavior. Only the president can be guilty for that. For the same reason, it's important to distinguish the Christian doctrine of original sin from the claim that all humans are guilty of what the first people did. They're not. Though it's true that all humans fell into sin with the sins of Adam and Eve, it is not true that all humans are guilty of what the first humans did. The nature of guilt precludes that possibility.

Not so with shame and honor. These conditions are communicable and contagious. I can become an object of social discrediting merely by means of association with others who themselves have suffered discrediting. The shame of those with whom I associate infects me. And the closer my perceived relationship to the shamed, the more pronounced my shame will be as a consequence of theirs. The same is true of honor. I can get a bump in social credit merely by way of perceived association with someone of high social standing. My increase in social standing will be a function of the perceived proximity of my association and the degree to which my associate is honored. If the honorable one identifies with me in a particularly strong way, my increase in honor will be all the more pronounced.

To see that this is true, imagine two images of you going viral on the internet. Let's say the first is a picture of you laughing over a casual lunch in the home of someone who has, in the years since that picture was taken, now come to be widely recognized as an outspoken white supremacist. You would likely worry about that picture. Even if you vehemently reject white supremacy, you'd still worry (with good reason) that you would suffer social discrediting as a consequence of the picture's having gone viral. And the appreciation of that fact would be painful. In that case, you will have "caught" the dishonor and shame of the white supremacist merely by association. Let's say the second picture is of you laughing over a casual lunch in the home of Jorge Mario Bergoglio (his name before he was more commonly known as Pope Francis). Likely you'd derive some positive feeling—felt honor—from the bump in social credit (the honor) that would be yours merely because of your perceived proximity to the honorable position of the pope. Honor and shame are contagious.

Because shame and honor are contagious in this way, felt shame has the unique function of creating communities of mutual interest and investment. If you and I are associates, then I can "catch" your shame and your honor merely by association. As a consequence, I will be invested in your acquisitions of shame and honor in a way that I could never be invested in your guilt or innocence. If I care about you, I *care* about your guilt and innocence. But because your guilt and innocence do not make me guilty or innocent, I'm not

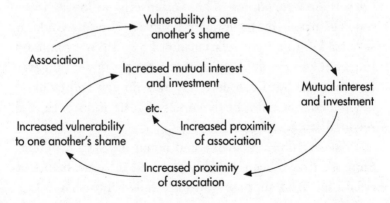

invested in your guilt or innocence *in the same way* as I am in your shame and honor. My shame and honor are intimately connected with yours, so I am invested in your shame and honor.

Since I can catch your shame and honor—since my own social standing is partially a function of yours—shame and honor bind me to you in a special way. This is true whether or not I love (or even like) you. The closer our perceived association, the more invested I will be. And since I am invested in your shame and honor, I'll posture myself differently toward you. Since my honor and shame are partly a consequence of yours, I'll invest myself differently in your acquisitions and losses of social standing. These investments of mine will, no doubt, bring us into greater relational proximity. We will, as a consequence of our investments in each other, be closer associates. This closer association will mean we're even more likely to catch each other's shame and honor. This increasing vulnerability to each other's shame and honor will generate greater mutual investment and interest. And so on.

The dynamics by which shame and honor bind us together into communities of ever-increasing mutual interest and investment are illustrated in the following cycle:

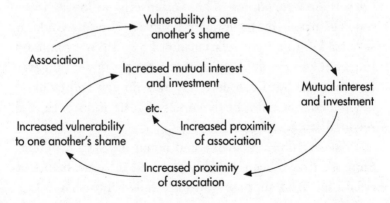

The contagious nature of shame also explains why the social dynamics of shame and honor differ from those of guilt and innocence. In particular, the path out of shame looks very different from the path out of guilt.

Imagine I am guilty of harming or wronging you in some way. Suppose my felt guilt is sufficient to motivate attempted reparation and reconciliation. Ordinarily, I, as the guilty party, can take certain steps to make things right—to assuage the felt guilt I feel for what I've done. For starters, I might apologize and seek to atone for what I've done. You may or may not forgive me. That's not up to me. So a reconciled relationship with you will never be entirely in my control. Often enough, though, I can repent, apologize, and make reparation for what I've done, whether or not I receive forgiveness as a consequence.

These acts of repentance, apology, and reparation will not render me innocent, of course. I'll never be innocent of the offense. What's done is done. But I can find my way back to something like a moral high ground all on my own. We don't say people are "innocent" when they've apologized, made ample reparation, and sought reconciliation to the best of their ability. But we do say they've dealt with their wrongdoing. Their offense is no longer to be held against them. Even if you forgive me and we find our way back into a right relationship, I am still not rendered innocent as a result. Again, what's done is done. I'll never be innocent, but I can be forgiven. And you and I can be reconciled. Such are the dynamics of guilt, innocence, and reconciliation.

The dynamics of shame and honor are very different. Suppose I have been publicly exposed in some shameful condition. And suppose you have fallen into shame as a consequence of your association with me. What are your options for escaping the shame you're experiencing? If you and I are not closely associated, you might be able to disassociate from me and thereby find some relief from the shame. But if you and I are closely associated (if, for example, I am your father), this path of disassociation may not be readily available. Often there is simply nothing you can do to prevent the social free fall that happens because of your close association with someone who has been shamed.

The same will be true if your shame comes as a consequence of a condition over which you have no control. If you suffer shame, for example, because of a publicly discernible impairment or disability, no obvious path will be available to lead you out of the shame you experience. This is why shame (unlike guilt) is often accompanied by feelings of helplessness and impotence. Often, it seems, there's nothing to do but hide.

There is one reliable path out of shame. But unlike the paths that remedy guilt (repentance, apology, and attempted reparation), it is not one that the person undergoing shame can undertake. This path must be pursued by someone *else* on behalf of the person suffering shame.

To envision this path, think of social credit as a kind of commodity. Some people have a high standing in society and have a lot of social credit. Others, for reasons that may or may not have to do with anything they've done, have a low standing in society. They do not have much by way of social credit. What we've seen so far is that social credit—social standing—is contagious. And unlike guilt and innocence, social credit *can* be transferred by mere association. If I have low social credit, your social credit can be diminished merely by association with me. And if

I have high social credit, yours can increase for no other reason than that you have been associated with me. These transactions of social credit are constantly occurring. People undergo increases and decreases of social standing every day—often by means of their associations with others. These transactions occur whether or not we take notice of them. And if you are highly attuned to shame and honor, you *do* take notice.

The reliable path out of shame, then, is by way of association with someone who has a high social credit score. When a person of high social standing condescends to identify with someone lower on the social totem pole, two things happen at once. The first is that the one who condescends suffers shame. Since low social standing is contagious, the one who condescends experiences a debit in their social credit balance. Depending on their balance at the time of the transaction, this may or may not be a cause of significant emotional disturbance. The second thing that happens is that the one who is lower on the social totem pole experiences an increase—a credit—in their social credit balance. They are honored—lifted out of shame. The degree to which they are lifted out of shame will be a function of the social credit score of the one who condescends and the degree of proximity achieved by the association. If the one who condescends is quite honorable indeed and the proximity achieved in the act of condescension is quite close, then the one suffering shame will be lifted significantly (even entirely) out of their shame. If you've ever talked to a junior higher about their experiences at school, you know all of this already. By mere association with the popular girl, the loner is lifted out of her shame. The popular girl suffers an initial decrease in standing when she's seen with the loner. But if she's popular enough, the loss will be insignificant. And the increase in status enjoyed by the loner will far exceed whatever losses were sustained by the popular girl.

Here, then, is another way in which shame (unlike guilt) binds us together into communities of mutual interest and investment. While I can ordinarily affect some degree of escape from the guilt I experience by means of repentance, apology, and attempted reparation and reconciliation, I am often powerless to affect escape from my shame. The escape from shame requires the cooperation of others—in particular, those with honor who are willing to condescend to suffer the shame of identification with me. My shame, unlike my guilt, renders me utterly dependent on the gracious condescension of honorable others.

This vulnerability to the gracious condescension of the other is anathema, of course, to someone in the grip of the ideal of self-sufficiency. This is why guilt (as ugly and uncomfortable as it is) is perfectly at home in the context of our Western, post-Enlightenment, radical individualism. The path out of guilt is available for me to pursue, whatever anyone else may or may not do, think, or feel. But the path out of shame is not ultimately available to me alone. It requires the gracious cooperation of others. I am not self-sufficient when I need to escape from shame and felt shame. I am dependent on those whom God has given me to share life with. Insofar as the ideal of self-sufficiency grips us, it is no wonder that we have a hard time appreciating the value of shame. But if we instead hold tightly to the ideal of progress toward increasing interest, investment, and identity with a community of others, then the valuation of shame makes perfect sense.

Similarities between Shame and Guilt

Now that we've contrasted the social dynamics of guilt and innocence and shame and honor, I'll close this chapter by highlighting a deep similarity between these two dimensions of our emotional experience. Recall that felt guilt and felt shame are both warning systems. The first alerts us to moral failure. The second alerts us to social discrediting. Both are uncomfortable, sometimes profoundly so. Sometimes these warning systems engage in such a way as to make focusing on anything else nearly impossible. And each is capable of going haywire. The victim of chronic guilt is persistently plagued by the painful emotional experience of having done something wrong—whether or not she has, in fact, done anything wrong. The victim of chronic shame is constantly troubled by the painful emotional experience of being worthless in the eyes of respectable others—whether or not he is, in fact, perceived as worthless.

If someone you love has been the victim of chronic shame or chronic guilt, you will, no doubt, be familiar with the temptation to be of assistance by disabling these warning systems. And if you've achieved any degree of success in disabling these systems, you'll likely have experienced the satisfaction that comes when you've relieved a beloved other from significant pain. It's a relief to have the painfully annoying warning light disabled. But I hope you can begin to see that the disabling of these systems is not the path to wholeness or health.

If a smoke detector goes off in your kitchen, your first reaction should not be to disable the fire alarm (however painful and disruptive it is). Your first reaction should be to look for a fire, then, should you find one, to put it out. Even if there is no fire, that's still no reason to permanently disable the smoke detector. Instead, you should try to identify and address whatever signaled the detector. Perhaps you've been a little too aggressive in your preparation of bananas Foster for dessert. In that case, you'll open windows and fan the room. If you determine that the smoke detector is going off indiscriminately, you still shouldn't disable it permanently. After all, smoke detectors are important. Instead, you'll want to take steps to *regulate* your smoke detector so that it is more sensitive to the facts on the ground. You'll want to fix it so that it sounds the alarm when (and only when) there is a fire.

If someone you love feels guilty for something they've done and you want to help, don't try to disable their ability to feel guilt. Instead, give them ideas for how to make apology and reparation for what they've done. Help them forge a path in the direction of reconciliation. You now recognize that if they take these steps toward reconciliation, their feelings of guilt should diminish. Even if someone you love feels constantly and persistently guilty, whether or not they have done anything wrong and regardless of their apologies and attempted reparations, you shouldn't try to disable their ability to feel guilt. Rather, you should try to help them *regulate* their feelings of guilt so that their feelings befit the facts. Help them to see and appreciate their own innocence when they are in fact innocent. And when they're guilty, help them to see and appreciate the degree to which they have already dealt with their guilt by means of repentance and apology.

The same is true of shame. If someone you love feels shame and you want to help, your first impulse should not be to disable their ability to feel shame. It should be to determine whether the shame they're experiencing is a consequence of something they can control. Perhaps the shame is from a simple failure of etiquette, or maybe it is from a gross and ongoing public moral failure. If so, you can seek to help them into the kind of conformity with moral and community standards that will give them relief from the shame they're experiencing. If their felt shame is a consequence of something they can't control (perhaps they have a publicly discernible disability), you'll still not want to disable their ability to feel shame altogether. Instead, you'll want to honor them. If you're in a position of honor, you'll condescend in such a way as to identify with them so that they can partake of your high social standing. If you're not in a position to honor them, you should advocate for social change to eliminate the social stigma associated with their condition. Even if your loved one feels shame indiscriminately—if they are persistently plagued by the feeling that they are poorly regarded, whether or not they are—your ultimate objective should not be to disable their ability to feel shame. Not unless you're in the grip of the post-Enlightenment Western ideal of complete self-sufficiency. Instead, you should point them to resources for *regulating* their experience of shame so that their feelings of shame befit the facts on the ground.

Both felt guilt and felt shame are important warning systems. Both alert us to conditions that detract significantly from human flourishing. The former alerts us to departures from innocence. The latter alerts us to social discrediting and dishonor. Both felt shame and felt guilt, when unregulated, can be harmful. In severe cases, they can be life-disrupting.

The conception of human flourishing that naturally accompanies a radical individualistic mindset makes it harder to comprehend the place of shame in healthy human psychologies and communities. If the idea is to make progress toward complete self-reliance and self-validation, then it'll be hard to make sense of the preservation of a painful warning system that alerts us to social discrediting. If, on the other hand, we think that people flourish most effectively when they are deeply interested and invested in the lives of those with whom they are in community, then it'll make perfect sense that there should be a warning system, hardwired in the human condition, that alerts us to social discrediting.

Shamelessness and radical individualism go hand in hand, as do the valuation of shame and pursuit of deep community.

CHAPTER 7

FROM SHAME TO SHAMING

So far our focus has been on shame and felt shame. We've not talked much about shaming as an activity. Recall that shame is the opposite of honor. You are honored in a community when you are lifted up—assigned greater weight, significance, or worth—in the eyes of that community. Similarly, you undergo shame in a community when you are dishonored or discredited in that community—when you are seen as less significant, worthy, or weighty in that community. If the community in question is one that matters to you, and if your emotions are aligned with what's happening, there will be feelings that accompany these gains and losses of social standing. If you are aware that you have been honored in a community that matters to you, a pleasant emotional response will be natural and fitting. You will *feel* honored. If you know you have been dishonored or shamed in a community that matters to you, an unpleasant emotional response will be apt. You will *feel* shame.

In these respects, the dynamics of honor and shame mirror those of guilt and innocence. If you are aware that your behavior transgresses a norm that matters to you, and if your emotions are aligned with what's happening, you will suffer an unpleasant emotional reaction. You will *feel* guilty. And if you are aware that your behavior is perfectly aligned with the norms that matter to you, you will enjoy *felt* innocence (or at least the absence of felt guilt).

In previous chapters I have argued that all these emotions, when regulated and aligned with the facts, have important work to do in healthy psychologies and communities. More specifically, I have argued that felt shame—once it is carefully distinguished from low self-esteem, self-loathing, and other failures of self-respect—makes an important contribution to the good life. I have been defending the nearly unanimous *positive* valuation of shame as found in the major wisdom traditions throughout human history.

In this chapter, we'll turn our attention to *shame* and *guilt* understood as verbs—to the *activities* of shaming and guilting people. When you guilt someone (or, as we sometimes say, "put them on a guilt trip"), your aim is to get them to *feel* something that they are not yet feeling (or not feeling as strongly as you'd like them to). Similarly, shaming is a matter of trying to make someone experience shame. When you shame someone, you're trying to generate the unpleasant emotion that accompanies the realization that you've been dishonored or discredited in the eyes of those who matter to you. And it's a seemingly natural step from the suggestion that shame and guilt are sometimes healthy (even if painful) dimensions of the good life to the thought that we'll sometimes need to help people into these painful experiences. If you are following closely, you might think it would sometimes be incumbent upon us to shame and guilt people.

Some of the confusion that animates contemporary

thinking about these topics can be seen in the relationship between recent attitudes toward shame on the one hand and shaming on the other. As we've seen, it is increasingly popular to think that shame is a toxic emotion and that we'd do well to eradicate it from the range of emotions that humans experience. Oddly enough, however, the activity of public shaming has been widely and visibly embraced today and is arguably more widespread than ever before. This prevalence is largely possible due to technological developments and the rise of social media, whereby public shaming has become a primary instrument of behavior modification and social change. Ironically, even as we denigrate shame as a toxic emotion, we seem to have wholeheartedly embraced shaming as a way of promoting social causes we care about. You don't need to scroll very far down your Facebook or Twitter feed to find naked, unabashed shaming in service of a wide variety of social causes. We're all familiar with some of the more visible and dramatic instances of extreme social discrediting in the service of a cause. Some of us may participate in this shaming, either with our own contributions to conversations that seek to discredit the parties involved or with our voracious appetite for these stories of social implosion. Shaming is alive and well today, even as shame has become increasingly anathematized. What's going on?

The Guilt Trip

Perhaps some further reflection on guilt-tripping will shed light on our embrace of shaming. For the most part, Western society frowns on guilt-tripping. At its worst, it's an instrument of raw manipulation. I want you to give to my nonprofit, and I can see that you're not strongly motivated to give. So I will try to make you feel guilty for not giving, in order to change your behavior. Most of us frown on that kind of guilt trip. This is nothing more than preying on the emotions of others (even if it is in the service of a good cause).

But suppose you've been stealing money from the non-profit you work for. And you don't feel at all guilty about it. You've rationalized your behavior by reflecting on your own felt need for the money and the insignificance of the amounts relative to the organization's total budget. In this case, I might attempt to help you into some feeling of guilt for what you've been doing. Sometimes people don't feel the guilt that is *appropriate* for their actions. And helping them into something like an affective alignment can be an act of love. A guilt trip might be just what you need. It might bring your feelings into alignment with what's true. And those guilty feelings might motivate correction and reparation.

If guilt-tripping can be a powerful motivator, shaming can be even more so. People can sometimes be shamed into behavior modification—even when they can't be made to feel guilty. People who cannot be made to feel guilty for going to the grocery store without a face mask during a pandemic (perhaps because they are skeptical about the effectiveness of masks for preventing the spread of the virus) might still be shamed into wearing one. Even if they do not think going without a mask is a transgression of any sensible norm or rule, the threat of social discrediting, if strong enough, may be enough to get them to wear one. And if enough of the people they care about made it a regular practice to call them out publicly and shame them for going without a mask, most would, in time, succumb to the pressure. They might conclude that freedom from mask-wearing isn't worth the shame to which they are being subjected. Shame can be a powerful motivational tool.

Sometimes it is in the service of love that we cause another person pain in an attempt to correct them, protect them, or prevent them from harming others. This isn't a tool we should wield thoughtlessly. It's something to be careful about, to be sure. But it's easy to think of examples that we'd all accept. For example, I often speak to my children with the aim of helping them develop a healthy fear of danger. I warn them about the cliff's edge to protect them. And while fear is an unpleasant emotion, most parents understand that what I'm doing is done in love. If I suddenly find my children in imminent danger of falling, I may even accidentally bruise them or otherwise injure them in an aggressive attempt to pull them away from mortal danger. Similarly, loving people sometimes requires the willingness to cause pain. Shaming and guilt-tripping can be like that (though not always, of course). These are painful activities, so we'll want to be careful and wise in their deployment. But they are sometimes done in the service of love.

The Difference between Guilting and Shaming

There's an important difference, however, between shaming and guilting. And it should make us far more hesitant about shaming. I hope that reflection on this difference will make it clear that the contemporary patterns of thought about shame and shaming have things exactly backward. Recall that for the most part, Western culture has grown increasingly suspicious of shame (thinking it to be an inherently toxic emotion) while increasingly accepting of the activity of shaming (treating it as an acceptable and important instrument of social change). I would argue that we need to flip these around. We should be increasingly suspicious of shaming (recognizing that it is *rarely* done in the service of love) and increasingly accepting of shame (recognizing that it has important work to do in healthy psychologies and communities).

Let's take a closer look at the crucial difference between shaming and guilt-tripping. First, notice that when you put someone on a guilt trip, you do not cause them to *be* guilty. If I guilt-trip you, I am trying to generate the unpleasant emotional experience that accompanies the recognition that you're guilty. But I'm not doing that by generating the guilt itself. In the typical case, you are already guilty but you're not having the unpleasant emotional experience that should accompany that guilt. So I'm trying to bring your emotions into alignment with what is already true. You're guilty. But you don't feel guilty. So I'm trying to help you into those feelings.

But a typical case of shaming works very differently. Imagine that John, a socially prominent member of his community, is engaged in some deplorable and harmful behavior that nobody knows about. Suppose I discover John's secret and publicly call him out. The shaming catches fire with the Twitter mob, and before long John's social standing plummets. He becomes, in a matter of hours, an object of public dishonor and scorn. John experiences the emotional pain that accompanies the recognition that he's been thoroughly discredited in society that matters to him. He has been successfully shamed. And he feels the sting of it.

When I guilt-trip someone, I cause them to feel guilty. But I don't cause this feeling by causing them to *be* guilty.

They were, presumably, guilty before I put them on the guilt trip. When I shame someone, I cause them to feel shame by causing them to *be* an object of shame. I bring about their social decline, and the painful experience of felt shame is the predictable consequence. When I put someone on a guilt trip, I am merely trying to bring their emotions into alignment with what is already the case (i.e., that they are guilty). When I shame someone, I am not merely trying to bring their emotions into alignment with what is already the case. In the most dramatic cases of shaming, what is true before the shaming is that the person is honored in a society that matters most to them. When I shame them, I am trying to bring about the reverse. I am trying not only to change the way the person feels but to bring about their social demise.

When shaming is used as an instrument of social change, the feelings of the person being shamed are rarely the primary object of concern. Shaming, in this context, is not aimed primarily at manipulating the feelings or behavior of the one being shamed. More often, the goal of the shaming has to do with the feelings and behavior of others. In John's case, we don't care so much about whether John feels the sting of social decline and corrects his behavior (though, of course, it'd be good if he did change his behavior). What we *really* want is for a lot of others to see John's social demise so they'll be less inclined to do the deplorable things John has done. If we shame enough people like John, fear of shame may result in fewer people doing what John did, affecting the social change we desire.

So, for all their apparent similarities, guilting and shaming are very *different* activities. When I guilt you, I deprive you of the pleasant experience of felt innocence. I cause you to have the painful experience of felt guilt. But I don't cause you to be guilty. And causing you to have this painful experience can be an expression of my love for you. I am trying to bring your feelings into alignment with what is true. And I'm trying to help guide you to better behavior so that you'll be guilty less often in the future. Shaming, on the other hand, is rarely a manifestation of love for the one shamed. It is rarely done with the person's good in mind. More often it is done with the good of others in mind. And it takes from the one shamed not only the pleasant experience of *feeling* like a valued member of society but also the person's positive standing in society itself.

It is for these reasons that shaming is far more difficult to justify than guilting. First, causing you pain that is for your own good is fairly easy to justify. If it weren't, dentistry would be an immoral industry. Causing you pain for the good of others is more difficult to justify. That's why torture for the prevention of terrorism *is* an immoral industry. Shaming, when not done as a manifestation of love for the person shamed, but in such a way as to use painful and harmful treatment of one person for the good of others, will be far more difficult to justify than the typical guilt trip.

Second, the harms associated with public shaming are different from those associated with guilt trips. When I put you on a guilt trip, the harm that I cause is entirely a matter of changing your feelings. I deprive you of your felt innocence, and I try to cause the painful feeling of guilt. Whether that's genuinely in the service of love will depend on whether the end or goal that I'm promoting for you is sufficient to warrant causing that particular painful feeling.

But when I publicly shame you, I don't just deprive you of pleasant feelings and cause you painful feelings. I deprive you of your standing in the company of respected others (whether or not you feel it). If the shaming is thoroughgoing (as it often is when it is in the service of a passionate cause), it will deprive you of membership in this community altogether. You will be thought a monster or a person of little consequence and will suffer the rejection of those who matter to you.

Since it is never in a person's interest to be thought a monster or to have no significance in the eyes of respectable others, it's difficult to conceive of thoroughgoing public shaming as a manifestation of love for the person shamed— even if it serves the interest of a loving cause, broadly conceived. So if you're committed to loving everyone to the best of your ability, it's much harder to justify publicly shaming someone instead of settling for a good old-fashioned guilt trip.

Private Shaming

But what about private shaming? If you're stealing money from the nonprofit you work for and I want to help you into greater integrity, I might start by trying to get you to experience the guilt that is appropriate, given what you've been up to. I might talk with you about ethical and biblical injunctions against stealing and dishonesty more generally. But what if I can't get you to feel guilty for what you're doing? What if you're so deeply invested in your rationalizations that you're incapable of appreciating your own wrongdoing? In that case, my attempts to get you to feel anything like guilt for what you're doing will fall flat. Still, shame might do the trick.

I might invite you to imagine others in the organization

discovering your behavior. Picture what would happen to your social standing in the organization (and beyond) if the light were to shine brightly on these financial transactions. Even if you're convinced that you're doing nothing wrong, the fear of imagined discovery and the resulting dishonor that would be yours should your actions be discovered, might result in a change of course. If so, and if a change of course is in the interest of your flourishing, then I would have loved you by *privately* shaming you—by causing you to have the unpleasant emotional experience of imagined social discrediting.

In his first letter to the Corinthian church, the apostle Paul invokes shame on several occasions in his attempt to affect pastoral correction. Apparently, the Christians in Corinth were not attuned to the shameful condition they were in. They professed to be followers of Jesus, the Prince of Peace. But they could not settle disputes with one another without taking each other to court to have those outside of Christ decide between them. There is a kind of ridiculousness about that—a ridiculousness that surely would have diminished the social standing of Christians in the larger community. But these Christians weren't feeling any of that. They were shameless. So Paul offers a vivid depiction of the foolishness of their condition. And he says these things to their shame (1 Corinthians 6:5).

Later (in chapter 15), Paul calls attention to the disconnect between the gospel message of resurrection power on the one hand and the Corinthian church's immorality and suspicion of bodily resurrection on the other. For Paul, it was clear that this disconnect made the whole Christian position—the Christian church—look like a ridiculous confusion. But apparently the Corinthians were not feeling the sting of having fallen into a position that was manifestly ridiculous. So he describes for them the foolishness into which they had slipped. And he does so to their shame (v. 34).

Private shaming, then, is more closely akin to putting someone on a guilt trip. It is not focused on causing shame or dishonor. It focuses instead on causing felt shame or the fear of felt shame by invoking *imagined* shame—imagined social discrediting. For this reason, the attempt to invoke felt shame privately is far easier to justify than public shaming. The feeling of shame or the fear of it that is brought on by imagined shame is a painful experience. So being the cause of that kind of pain will require some justification. All things being equal, we think it a bad business to cause painful feelings in others. But it's easy to see, from the examples I've mentioned, how causing these feelings might very well be in someone's best interest.

But private shaming is not the sort of thing you do on Twitter, on a YouTube channel, or in a group conversation at a dinner party. It is something you do in a private conversation where nobody's *actual* social standing is at stake. If I shame you in public, I'll cause the painful experience of felt shame, but I'll also cause you to be shamed as a matter of fact. I will bring about your dishonor and cause you to be a person of lesser significance in the company of those you respect. That's a harm to you that goes beyond the painful emotional experience of felt shame. And it's more difficult to justify.

The reason that causing you to be dishonored is more difficult to justify has to do with the close connection between your own well-being and your being included and accepted in the company of respected others. As I noted before, we are essentially social creatures. As much as we promote a romantic attachment to rugged individualism, the old cliché is closer to the truth: nobody is an island. We all need connection and acceptance, and we need to belong. To deprive someone of their felt innocence by putting them on a guilt trip might make them uncomfortable, but it does not deprive them of something essential to their well-being. Yet when we take from someone the possibility of belonging to their community—when we reduce them to the status of a monster or an alien—we take from them something essential to their well-being, something as essential as food and water.

Complete and thoroughgoing public shaming will almost never be justifiable for a person committed to an ethic of universal or Christian love—an ethic that requires us to love everyone, including the enemies of our most cherished social and political causes. For someone who thinks that larger causes can sometimes override the duty to love every individual, this kind of thoroughgoing public shaming might occasionally find legitimate expression. But we should all agree that it is very difficult to justify the complete undoing of a person for the sake of another (or some group of others). And we should agree that when we deprive someone of something so essential to their well-being as the possibility of belonging in the company of respected others—when we reduce them to the status of monster or alien—we do not love them. At best, we sacrifice them in an attempt to love others, and at worst, we sacrifice them to satisfy our felt need for vengeance.

But what about less extreme acts of public shaming? In my classes, I expect students to pay attention to the lecture as it's occurring and to take notes so they can prepare for exams. Occasionally, I interrupt my lecture to ask students what they think of a particular point I've made or to generate discussion around an important idea. If I notice a student who seems to be daydreaming, I'll sometimes call on that student and ask for some comment on what's just been said. I do this so that everyone in the class will be aware that the student is not paying attention. In other words, I publicly dishonor the student for not paying attention to cause in that student the emotional discomfort that comes from being publicly dishonored and to motivate that student and everyone else in the room to conduct themselves differently. This is public shaming pure and simple.

But it's public shaming in a relatively controlled environment. There's no real danger that, as a consequence of my behavior, the student will be considered a moral monster or an alien. There's no real threat that they will be excluded from the company of those they love and respect as a consequence of what I've done. In fact, if I'm sensitive to the dynamics of honor and shame, I'll be far less likely to call a student out like this if I think they have very little social capital to begin with—if I think this is a student with low social standing in the company of their peers. I'm more likely to do this to a student who can afford to be taken down a notch. Part of successfully facilitating group learning is the ability to level the social dynamics in the room so that participants with lower initial social standing can more effectively participate.

So it's not true that public shaming is always and everywhere something frowned upon. There is a place for it. But we need to recognize that when we publicly shame someone, the stakes are higher than when we privately shame them or when we put them on a guilt trip. That's because we're not simply acting to affect the *feelings* of the person we're shaming. We're also taking something from them that is essential to their flourishing. We are acting in such a way as to take away their honor and standing in their community. And if that's to be done, it should be done in controlled environments. To state the obvious, Twitter and Facebook (or any social media platform) are not controlled environments.

So is legitimate public shaming possible? That will depend on the answers to questions like these: Can you shame the person by taking them down a notch without removing them from social standing in their community? In other words, can the shaming be controlled? Or will this act of public shaming result in further acts of shaming, making it difficult to control the degree of shame this person will experience? In short, is this act of public shaming consistent with my goal of loving the person shamed? To the degree that public shaming is difficult to control, it will also be far more challenging to justify unless you're willing to sacrifice the flourishing of the one being shamed for the sake of some larger cause. But that means abandoning an ethic of Christian love.

Even if shaming is done privately, we should take into account the potential harm we might cause to the person shamed and should therefore be cautious in how and when we utilize shame. Recall that when you guilt-trip someone, you take from nothing more than their felt innocence. As it turns out, we are pretty good at retaining our self-respect even when we lose our sense of felt innocence. We tell ourselves, "That was a bad business. I shouldn't have done that. I'm guilty. And I'm sorry. But I'm not a bad person. That was a slip. A mistake. Not a serious reflection of who or what I am." Since felt guilt is focused on a particular behavior and not on the self considered as a whole, it is easier to feel guilty without thinking of our self as a bad or evil person.

On the other hand, when we privately shame someone, we take from them the assurance that, were they really known by the people who matter most to them, those people would continue to think well of them. And we are not good at retaining our self-respect when we think we would be diminished in the eyes of those we love and respect. We tend to think, "Were this thing about me known by the people who matter most to me, they would think less of me. How could all these respectable people be wrong about a thing like that? They must be right. I must be a bad person." When I am dishonored, it is my whole self—my standing as a person in society—that suffers loss. And we are hardwired to accept the public perception of ourselves in communities that matter to us. So retaining a high view of ourselves is difficult when we are asked (even in private conversation) to imagine the dishonor that would be ours were we fully known by the people who matter most to us.

Our self-esteem is more vulnerable to dishonor—even imagined dishonor—than it is to recognized guilt. And because of this, we are more likely to fall into failures of self-respect as a consequence of shaming (even when done in private) than as a consequence of being put on a guilt trip. Felt shame, even when it is not confused with self-dislike, negative self-evaluation, or low self-esteem, is a more potent cause of failed self-respect than is felt guilt.

Shaming: A Cautious Approach

So here is where we land: *Even if there is nothing inherently wrong with or unhealthy about felt shame, there are good reasons to be extremely suspect of shaming as an activity.* Shame has important work to do in healthy psychologies and communities. But that doesn't mean we should routinely take it upon ourselves to shame people. Felt shame, like felt guilt, does not typically require a third party to help it into existence. Most people have a conscience. They *feel* guilty when they know they *are* guilty. No guilt trip is required. And most people have a sense of shame. They *feel* socially discredited when they have *been* socially discredited. No shaming is required.

Sometimes people do not feel what would be apt for them to feel in context. They don't *feel* guilty when they *are* guilty. Or they don't feel shame when they have been shamed, dishonored, or otherwise socially discredited in communities that matter to them (or would be discredited were they truly known). In these cases, we may be tempted to help them toward affective alignment. Yet even here we should keep in mind that affective alignment is not always the most pressing goal. If your best friends have abandoned you, but you're not feeling sharply the pain of betrayal and loneliness, that may very well be a consequence of God's gracious protection. God may be protecting you from feeling the full pain of loneliness. And I'm not sure it would be the most loving thing to help you in the direction of affective alignment—to help you experience the severity of emotional pain apt for having been abandoned by your closest companions. As with anything, we must exercise wisdom and good judgment. Affective alignment must be weighed in the balance against other good ends that we try to bring to those we love.

There may be occasions when causing felt guilt or felt shame is in the most loving thing we can do. This is true even when the emotion you bring about is painful, since love will sometimes necessitate causing others pain. But when that's the case, it's always because the positive value of what you're trying to bring about overrides the negative value of the pain you're causing. The focus of this chapter has been to show that the negative value of the pains associated with both public and private shaming are significant. They are typically greater than the negative value of the pain associated with being made to feel guilty and bring their emotions into affective alignment. So it is difficult to justify *any* act of public or private shaming—far more difficult than justifying an attempt to make someone feel guilty for what they've done. So long as we are committed to an ethic of Christian love—of showing no preference in who we love, even toward our enemies—we should be very slow to participate in the kind of public shaming that animates many of the social movements of our day. To put it bluntly, someone who claims to follow the ethic of Christian love should rarely, if ever, utilize the practice of shaming. Given its uniquely destructive power to untether the victim from their own sense of self-worth, it is rarely compatible with the teachings of Jesus.

CHAPTER 8

CONCLUSIONS AND APPLICATIONS

The central claim of this book has been that the dominant movement in contemporary Western culture has things exactly backward when it comes to shame. In psychology, counseling, the social sciences, and even popular culture, the contemporary Western mindset is decidedly *antishame*. It contends that shame is an inherently destructive emotion and that we should eliminate it from the range of emotions we experience. Ironically, shaming, on the other hand, has been widely embraced as an acceptable instrument of social change. It is explicitly embraced by those who seek the public disgrace of others for the sake of their cause or movement. And it is tacitly embraced by the rest of us who have an appetite for the consumption of stories about folks who have been successfully shamed. Ours is a culture that is extremely suspicious of shame but widely accepting of shaming.

This is what I mean when I say we have things *exactly backward*. We should be far more suspicious of shaming than we are. And we should be far less suspicious of felt shame.

We should be more suspicious of shaming because shaming is rarely an expression of love. More often, shaming is an expression of the need for vengeance, an act motivated by a desire for retribution or hatred of another. And even when it is done as an expression of love, it is rarely an expression of love for the one shamed. More often, the well-being of the one shamed is sacrificed for the good of others to promote a particular cause.

Acts of public and private shaming *can*, in limited and controlled circumstances, be expressions of love for the one shamed. They *can* be done in such a way as to promote the well-being of the one shamed. So I'm not arguing for an absolute prohibition on public or private shaming. But the harms inflicted in an act of shaming are exceedingly difficult to control, and they often have destructive consequences beyond the felt shame of the one shamed. Because the human need for social standing and connection in community is so deep and so central to well-being, any attempt to diminish the social standing of another flirts with the possibility of undermining the other's well-being. And because we take our cues from the important others in our lives when we are formulating our self-identity, any attempt to diminish a person's sense of how others perceive them flirts with the possibility of undermining their own self-respect.

Inflicting harm *is*, we've noticed, sometimes done in the service of love—often because it serves to prevent a greater harm. But harms that are difficult to control—harms that easily devolve into utterly destructive realities for the person harmed—are more difficult to justify. We ought to be suspicious and cautious when we consider inflicting harms of that sort. And that means we should generally reject the act of shaming and move in a direction contrary to our contemporary culture.

On the other hand, I've argued that we should be less suspicious of felt shame. In its healthy expressions, felt shame is the painful experience of a potentially destructive reality. It is precisely because being subject to shame—being discredited in the company of those who matter to us—is so potentially destructive that we are fitted with a painful emotional response to it. As we have seen, the emotional experience of shame alerts us that we have been socially discredited in the same way that the emotional experience of loneliness alerts us that we are without companionship or the feeling of betrayal alerts us to the absence of fidelity in our relationships. Only someone who thought companionship and fidelity unimportant would be interested in eliminating the ability to feel lonely or betrayed. Similarly, it would make sense to eliminate your ability to feel shame only were it unimportant to be accepted, connected, and well regarded in communities that matter to you.

Eliminating the ability to feel shame makes sense for many today only because we live in the context of the most extreme versions of individualism. Today's radical individualism severs the connection between well-being and belonging in a community of mutual respect. Yes, the painful emotions of betrayal, loneliness, and shame can express themselves in unhealthy ways. And these painful emotions, when unregulated, can contribute significantly to psychological unhealth. This is all true. But the goal should be to move in the direction of their healthy, regulated expression, not to eliminate the ability to feel them when they are apt. None of these emotions are *inherently* toxic or unhealthy. The increasingly popular tendency to think of shame, in particular, as inherently toxic owes largely to the failure to distinguish felt shame from the common causes of unhealthy expressions of felt shame: low self-esteem, self-loathing, and other failures of self-respect. The opposite of shame is not self-respect. It is honor. And honor can be acquired by someone with little or no self-respect and lost without any corresponding loss of self-respect.

Shame and Honor in the Prodigal Son Story

Once you know what to look for, the categories of shame and honor are all throughout the Bible. This should not surprise us, given that the human authors of the Scriptures were, without exception, writing from cultural perspectives heavily influenced by shame and honor dynamics. My favorite biblical picture of the shame and honor dynamic comes to us in the story that Jesus tells about the so-called prodigal son. The younger of two brothers convinces his father to advance him his share of the inheritance, which he then squanders on wild living and prostitutes. When a famine hits and the son can't support himself, and after stooping to the level of pigs to get food for sustenance, he decides to return to his father. Humiliated and defeated, the son thinks himself unworthy to return as a son and hopes merely to be taken in as a servant. The father sees him coming from afar, has compassion on him, runs to him, embraces him, kisses him, and (much to the frustration of the older brother) throws a feast in his honor, puts a ring on his finger, and dresses him in his finest robes.

For the longest time, I read this as a story about the free gift of unconditional forgiveness bestowed by a loving father on the son who had wronged him. The father forgives his son unconditionally, offers him no punishment, accepts him without qualification, and restores him to a place of right relationship.

But what is there, exactly, for the father to forgive? Did the son wrong his father in any way? It is the son who declares to his father that he has sinned, not only against God but also against his father. But the son is not exactly the trustworthy voice in this story. Can we, the readers, identify anything that the son has done to harm or wrong the father? Anything that would require the father's forgiveness? He didn't steal the money. It was his. The father had given it to him. So, presumably, it was his to squander. What he did was foolish, to be sure. And it was immoral (insofar as his wild living was in violation of moral purity). But how, exactly, is that a sin against his father? Why would he need his father's forgiveness for that? And why is there no mention at all in the story of the father forgiving the son? The father runs to him, embraces him, kisses him, rings his finger, and celebrates his return. He does much to *honor* his son. But the concept of forgiveness makes no explicit appearance in the story. When the *father* tells the son's story, there is no mention of the son's having wronged him. Nor is there any mention of the father forgiving the son or foregoing just punishment. In the father's telling, the story is about someone lost being found—someone dead being made to live again. It is not, in any obvious way, a story about someone in the wrong being forgiven—someone deserving of punishment being spared.

What the story goes out of its way to make obvious is that the son had fallen into shame. His foolish course had brought him from a position of reasonably high social standing down to the level of the pigs. And it's clear that he felt the sting of the social discrediting that had come his way.

He no longer considered himself worthy to be called his father's son. So he had fallen into shame, and he, no doubt, felt the humiliating sting of felt shame.

How does the father respond? Not by acknowledging the wrongdoing and extending forgiveness. The father never affirms the son's description of what went down. But neither does the father tell the son that he's wrong or unhealthy to feel the shame he feels. There's no indication here that the father thought it inappropriate or unhealthy for the son to feel the sting of his shameful condition. Instead, the father's response to the son's shame is to publicly restore his honor. The way the story is told makes it as plain as can be that the restoration of honor is at the center of the father's response. And, importantly, the rescue from shame did not come through the indictment of the son's felt shame as an unhealthy or toxic emotional response to the son's condition. The rescue from shame came through the restoration of honor.

The first thing the father does is to run to his son. For the audience that Jesus was addressing (and for many cultural audiences still today), this detail sends a clear signal. The father is setting aside his dignity and his honor in the way he approaches his son. Dignified men do not run. The picture of a man running in his robes to embrace his dishonored son communicates that the man is setting aside his honor and condescending to his disgraced beloved. Then the father embraces and kisses his son, declaring to everyone watching that he and his son are united. He identifies with his son, saying, in effect, "He's with me!" This would have further dishonored the father—remember that shame is contagious. If you fall into shame and I strongly identify with you, I'm likely to fall into shame myself. Were the father concerned with the preservation of his honor, he would have publicly disowned his son. He could have forgiven him, refraining from punishment or hard treatment, while still making it clear that he did not identify with his disgraced son.

Instead, he condescends to embrace his dishonored son, and he symbolizes their unity by putting a ring on his finger. The goal of the story is to showcase the father's willingness to suffer the indignity of identifying with his dishonored son. The father endures dishonor by condescending to his son to lift him out of shame. The story ends with feasts and with the father clothing his dishonored son in robes, an indication that he has restored his son to a place of honor in the father's household.

The primary message of the story is not that of a son who wrongs his father and receives generous unconditional forgiveness rather than punishment. It is a story about a son who falls into shame and is restored to honor by a father willing to condescend and suffer indignity by identifying with and celebrating the dishonored son. That's the way shame and honor work. If I have fallen into shame—if I have become a person of little consequence (or worse) in respectable society—there's usually nothing I can do to affect my own rescue. What I need is for someone with a high social standing (someone honored in respectable company) to strongly identify with me.

If you are of low standing and you are seen casually strolling and laughing with the pope through the city of Rome, folks might scratch their heads and wonder what he's doing with the likes of you. But the social increase you experience will far outweigh whatever social decrease comes his way because of the association. The pope has a lot of social capital to spare. He has the powerful ability to honor people simply by means of casual association. Imagine what people would think of you were the pope to see you from afar, break into a sprint (robes and all), embrace and kiss you, put his ring on your finger, and then throw a feast in your honor.

When we read the prodigal son story as a picture of the incarnation and atonement, we find it has less to say about the *forgiveness* freely available to us in Christ and far more about God's plan for rescuing us from the *shame* of our fallen condition. We, like the son, have fallen into shame as a consequence of sin. And when you have fallen far into shame, nothing you do can restore your own honor. You're stuck, unless someone with honor to spare is willing to condescend to identify with you. In the incarnation, when God became a human being, Christ suffered the indignity of identifying with the shamed, like the father in the story. He says, in effect, "I'm with them." And he condescends not only to become a man but also to suffer the shame of betrayal, wrongful conviction, torture, and naked crucifixion to rescue human beings from their fallen condition. He promises a feast of celebration for all who receive his gracious offer of rescue.

I often wish the prodigal son story had continued. Like a kid at the end of his bedtime story, I want to know what happened next. I imagine that the younger son, having been lifted out of his shame, goes on to become a powerful force for the good of his family and his community. Perhaps, having experienced the want of famine, he goes on to devise techniques and technology for protecting his family and community from the destructive effects of famine in the future. Perhaps his future activities elevate him further in the community, and as his honor increases, so does his father's. Whatever dishonor the father suffered as a consequence of identifying with his shamed son is likely outweighed by the honor he now receives as the father of the community's hero.

That's how I'd *like* to think the story ends. In any case, that is the promised ending to the grand drama of human history. We who have fallen into shame have our honor restored through our association with Jesus Christ, who graciously condescended to identify with our plight. But that's not all. We go on to reign victorious with Christ over the redeemed created order. And God is glorified by the whole story. The victorious redemption of the human race vindicates God's gracious condescension. Human beings are not only rescued from their own shame, they are *rendered capable of bringing honor and glory to their Creator.* The shame Christ endured in his sacrificial, condescending identification with fallen humanity is outweighed by the glory God receives as humanity assumes its intended role as the steward of God's redeemed creation. As the apostle Paul puts it in 2 Corinthians 4, we are raised up with Christ, which results in God's glory. And our momentary afflictions produce an eternal weight of glory beyond all comparison. It is those brought lowest by the shameful condition of the human race with whom Christ seems most eager to identify. The message is clear. God, in the condescending work of Christ, brings honor to the shamed. And they, in return, are made capable of bringing glory to God.

Shame and Honor in the Adam and Eve Story

The categories of shame and honor deepen our understanding of the beginning of the biblical story as well. In one man, Adam, the entire human race fell into a condition from which it would need the gracious redemption of God. Obvious puzzles arise when you try to understand this doctrine of original sin in terms of guilt, innocence, and forgiveness. How can anyone but Adam be guilty for what he did? How can anyone but Adam need forgiveness for what he did? We can understand how Adam's sin would infect the human race with a kind of brokenness and dysfunction. We know that brokenness and dysfunction of all kinds can be passed along through the generations. Brokenness and dysfunction can be inherited. They are contagious. But guilt is not contagious. As we saw in previous chapters, I can be guilty only for what I have done. So why would I need redemption because of what Adam did? Why not simply healing?

One part of the answer to this question is found by applying the categories of shame and honor to our reading. The story of humanity's fall is one of descent into shame. The themes of embarrassed nakedness, withdrawal, and hiding make it clear that the condition of Adam and Eve after the fall included not only guilt for having disobeyed God but also shame. Adam and Eve brought dishonor to themselves in their act of disobedience. And they brought dishonor to God, who had created them and assigned them stewardship over the created order. Importantly, they brought dishonor to their children and to the generations of children to follow. Their guilt may not have been transmissible. But their shame was.

Though I cannot be guilty for what my father does, I can certainly fall into shame because of what he does. And I can feel the sting of that shame—the social discrediting I've experienced because of what my father has done—even if I know I played no part in my father's offense. In the same way, an entire country can fall into shame in the international community when its leader is widely considered to have engaged in shameful behavior. Shame, unlike guilt, is contagious and can be inherited. So there's no mystery in the idea that the entire human race fell into a state of shame by means of the disobedience of Adam and Eve. It's not simply that we are broken and dysfunctional because of the inherited effects of the disobedience of others (though no doubt that's true). And it's not just that we need forgiveness because of our own acts of disobedience (though no doubt that's true as well). It's that we have fallen into a condition of inescapable shame as a consequence of the shameful disobedience of others—Adam and Eve. And having fallen into shame, as we have through their disobedience, we *should* feel the sting of that shame and *should* desire and seek not only forgiveness but also rescue from shame.

What about "White Shame"?

As a white man living in Orange County, California, I am sometimes confronted with the question of whether I should feel a sense of shame for my ethnicity or for the color of my skin. Is so-called white shame something that should enter into my experience, were my emotions properly attuned to my circumstances? It's tempting to answer the question too quickly and defensively say, "Of course not! There's nothing shameful about being white." I'm not, best I can tell, guilty of the kind of egregious racial prejudice, mistreatment, and outright abuse that has led to such deplorable racial inequities in our context. If you traced my ancestry, I have no doubt that you'd find much of that. But I've not been party to it. Some would argue that while there's every reason for me to stand with people of color and to fight with them for justice and equality, there's no reason for me to feel shame over what other white people have done.

But I warned that we should not be too quick to answer this question. Our initial, defensive response falsely presupposes that shame, like guilt, is something that can be yours only because of something you yourself have done. Imagine it's true that I'm innocent of egregious racial prejudice and of outright mistreatment and abuse of people of color. Suppose I endeavor to stand with people of color and to fight with them for justice and equality. It can also be true that when I reflect on my life, I recognize that many of the opportunities I've enjoyed have come as a consequence of prejudice and the mistreatment and abuse of others, especially those of other skin colors and ethnicities.

I recognize that my relative financial security, emotional stability, and advanced education, while owing in part to my own hard work, are significantly a consequence of the privileges that have come with being born a white man in the United States in the twentieth century. And I recognize that being a white man confers those privileges, in large measure, because of the purposeful exclusion, abuse, and mistreatment of women and people of color by white men for generations. I recognize, in other words, that my lot in life is not entirely a consequence of my own hard work and determination. My successes (such as they are) have a long and sordid history that began long before I was born.

How should I *feel* about that? Guilt seems squarely out of place. I am not guilty for having the ancestors, the gender, or the skin color I have. Diminished self-respect or self-loathing seem equally out of place. After all, I *have* worked hard. My education, for example, was not handed to me on a silver platter. I worked diligently for it. And if I didn't have to worry about sounding arrogant, I'd even say I'm proud of the hard work I've done and the education I've acquired.

Knowing that these opportunities have come to me in part by means of the abuse and mistreatment of others does not diminish my self-respect or the pride I feel in the work I've done. But what about shame? What about the painful experience of real or imagined social discrediting in the company of those who matter to me? As we've seen, that painful experience—the painful experience of felt shame—*can* accompany felt innocence and even healthy self-respect.

People who don't reflect carefully on the history of race and gender will be tempted to think that my lot in life has been entirely my own doing. They'll be tempted to think that everyone born in this country has the same basic opportunities—that anybody can be anything. So they'll be tempted to think that my own hard work and determination entirely explain my successes and that my own failures and shortcomings fully explain my deficiencies. I think I tacitly assumed this point of view for a long time. I don't think I would have put it quite that way, but I unconsciously assumed that everyone (or nearly everyone) could seize the same opportunities in life that have come my way.

I was wrong about that. And when I discovered I was wrong about it, that breakthrough was accompanied by the recognition that the people whose opinions matter most to me did not chalk up my successes entirely to my hard work and determination. They had recognized for a long time what was just dawning on me. They knew that a significant part of the explanation for my relative financial security, emotional stability, and level of education had nothing to do with me. They knew that these positive experiences are explained in part by the systematic exclusion, abuse, and mistreatment of others. Because of this, my voice in community conversations on matters of race and gender, I began to notice, was less highly esteemed—less authoritative—than it would otherwise be. My education being what it is, it was easy to grow accustomed to having an authoritative voice in community conversations. But in conversations about race and gender, the authority of my voice was taken down a notch. This view of my success and the authority of my voice was deflating. And I felt the sting of that deflation.

Being a white man, I have experienced the pain of diminished standing in the company of respectable others—shame—because of my privileged status and the wrongs others of privileged status have committed. Viewed in the light of this long history of targeted wrongdoing, my successes are less impressive. Not only are my successes not entirely the consequence of my own hard work and determination, they have come to me through a history of deplorable exclusion and abuse. And my failures are less excusable. When I have failed, I've failed despite having been blessed with inordinate opportunity for success. And the authority of my voice in community conversations about race and gender is palpably diminished. There is shame—even if no guilt and no diminishing of self-respect—in the recognition that my station in life is partly explained by my being white and male.

The shame I experience as a white man is nothing, of course, compared with the shame of having been mistreated and excluded in the ways that women and people of color have been for generations. In fact, when the subject is anything other than race or gender, my voice almost certainly continues to enjoy more authority than it is due, precisely because I am a white man. We have not yet moved beyond white male privilege. Juxtaposed against the intense shame women and people of color have experienced for generations, my experiences of shame as a white male are almost embarrassing to discuss. But these are experiences of shame nevertheless. Just as I suffer shame as a consequence of the disobedience of Adam and Eve, I suffer shame as a consequence of the systematic exclusion and abuse of others that partially explains my station in life as a white man. My shame is not simply a function of what I have and haven't done. Shame can come my way because of the socially diminishing conditions into which I was born. And my *felt* shame is the painful experience that accompanies the recognition of being so diminished.

In the case of the white shame I experience, I agree with the judgments that take me down a notch in communities that matter to me. I agree, that is, that my successes are less impressive and my failures are less excusable because of the inordinate opportunities for success afforded white men in our setting. And I agree that those who have suffered injustice should have a kind of authority in community conversations concerning those injustices—that I should do more listening and less talking in those conversations.

Sometimes, though, shame can come to us for reasons we do *not* endorse. We've seen that people with visible impairments and disabilities are taken down a notch for no other reason than that they have visible impairments or disabilities. And we've seen that if their emotions are attuned to the realities they're living with, they will feel the sting of that shame. It hurts to be an object of shame in the communities that matter most to you. It hurts even if you don't accept the standards that give rise to your shame. That particular hurt is felt shame. And it is not dysfunctional or unhealthy when the shame—the social discrediting—that befalls folks with visible disabilities is accompanied by the painful emotion of felt shame.

The Way out of This Dilemma

It is this painful experience of felt shame that motivates hiding. If you can mask or hide your disability, you'll avoid the painful sting of social discrediting. This is part of the reason why victims of sexual abuse, who are also routinely subjects of social discrediting, are often reluctant to tell their stories. Unlike having physical impairments, being a victim of sexual abuse is fairly easy to hide. You don't have to tell your story if you don't want to. And, tragically, if you tell your story, you will likely undergo shame. Even if you are not thought a liar and everyone believes you, you will tragically be diminished in society because of your status as a victim of sexual abuse. Sexual purity elevates social standing and sexual impurity (no matter whose fault) diminishes it. Strength and dominance over others elevate us, while weakness and victimhood diminish us. Of course, almost nobody *explicitly* endorses these ridiculous standards, just as almost nobody *explicitly* endorses a standard that would diminish folks for having visible impairments. But the standards are very much there nevertheless, and they are most palpably felt by the people who fall on the wrong side of them. Wherever possible, it's easier just to hide.

But if we've learned anything from psychologists who work in this area, it's that hiding often exacerbates the problem. It is precisely when I am so invested in hiding myself from communities that matter most to me that my felt shame is most likely to devolve into low self-esteem and other failures of self-respect. So here is the painful dilemma for you if you have an impairment or disability that can be hidden or a story of sexual abuse that you could keep to yourself: Hiding is not the path to health. Hiding will most likely make it more difficult to retain a healthy sense of yourself—to retain self-respect and healthy self-esteem. But self-revelation will bring about your shame—it will result in your being socially discredited. If your emotions are attuned to your reality, that will be painful. You will have the painful experience of felt shame. And we know that our sense of self is closely tied to how we feel about how others perceive us, especially those who matter most to us. So if you come out of hiding and feel the full force of the social diminishing that results, it'll be difficult to retain a healthy sense of yourself—to retain your self-respect and healthy self-esteem. Either way, whether you hide or not, you will likely struggle with self-esteem.

More than anything else, I think this is the dilemma that motivates the contemporary Western antishame zeitgeist. Were you to somehow be inoculated against felt shame, you'd have a way out of this dilemma. You could come out of hiding without feeling the pain associated with the social decline that would, given the standards currently in play, be yours as a result. And since you'd no longer feel the brunt of that social decline, you might find it more manageable to retain your own self-respect even though your standing among those who matter most to you is diminished. Perhaps you could somehow learn to completely self-validate—to sever the connection entirely between the experience of your self and the experience of your self as perceived by others. Or if you are a Christian, perhaps you could experience yourself—your self-worth and self-identity—based entirely on how God sees you.

Notice two things, though, about this way out of the dilemma. First, for better or worse, it is thoroughly individualistic. It represents an embrace of the ideal self entirely abstracted from the community of others. It idealizes the attempt to experience myself completely in my own terms (or perhaps as in God's terms as *I* understand God). So it represents a perspective of the self that departs from the global consensus of historical human wisdom (Christian and otherwise).

Second, and far more troubling, this way out of the dilemma suggests that it is felt shame—the emotionally painful experience of having been socially discredited—that is to blame for the psychological unhealth of folks who are shamed for their disabilities or for being victims of sexual abuse. But the *felt* shame of rape victims who tell their stories and are shamed as a result is *not* the problem. The problem is that they are shamed. The problem is that they are socially discredited for telling their stories. That they feel the pain of the shame that comes their way for having told their stories is simply an indication that their emotions are tracking the truth. There's something not only misguided but also reprehensible about the suggestion that it is wrong for them to feel the emotional pain of shame when they are, in fact, being shamed. It's the shaming that is wrong, not their experience of it. Let's not continue to seek the solution to the problem by assuming we must fix the victim.

If we want to help folks who feel shame because of their disability or because they've been sexually abused, we should take aim not at their felt shame but at the social conditions that give rise to their shame. It is *absurd* that rape victims and people with disabilities should have to hide who they are or what has happened to them to retain their status in their communities. If we want to help, we should attack the features of our communal life that downgrade folks on these grounds. In the meantime, we should give those who are suffering shame resources for retaining their own sense of self even as they experience the painful reality of social decline when they come out of hiding. To attack felt shame is to suggest that something about the emotional response of the abused or the disabled is most deeply to blame for their psychological unhealth. It isn't. It is the fact that society downgrades the disabled and abused that is most deeply to blame. The pain of felt shame that accompanies that downgrade is simply a manifestation of human emotions functioning as they were designed to.

Finally, we should consider the case of felt shame that is deserved. To this point, we've focused on cases where shame (and the corresponding felt shame) comes as a consequence of conditions for which the person shamed is not blameworthy (being white, being disabled, being a victim of sexual abuse). Sometimes, however, you experience shame because you've done something shameful.

To do something shameful is to do something that, if discovered, would result in your feeling shame in a well-functioning community. Having a disability is not shameful, yet it often results in shame in many of our communities. But that is because these communities are dysfunctional—they have disordered standards for assigning social significance to people. In a well-functioning community, having a disability would not result in shame. So having a disability is not shameful—no matter what community you're in. The person with a disability has nothing to be ashamed of even if they experience felt shame because they live in a community that shames them.

Being a perpetrator of sexual abuse, on the other hand, is shameful. In a well-functioning community, perpetrators of sexual abuse are socially discredited for what they've done. And if their emotions are tracking what's true, they will experience felt shame. They will feel guilt to the degree that they recognize their behavior to have violated a standard that they care about. And they will feel shame to the degree that they appreciate their social decline in communities that matter to them as a consequence of what they have done. Neither emotion would be unhealthy or out of place.

Four Shame Scenarios

So shame can come my way, whether or not I am in control of the circumstances that have given rise to my shame and whether or not I accept the reasons for my having been shamed. Note the following four scenarios.

I can experience shame for reasons that I accept but in circumstances over which I have no control. I have no control over the color of my skin. And I have nothing to be ashamed of on that score. But I accept the idea that my successes in life are less impressive, my failures less excusable, and my voice less authoritative on matters of race and gender because of the privileges associated with being a white man and because of the sordid history of those privileges. I am diminished in communities that matter to me for being a white man. And I feel the shame of being thus diminished even if I am not ashamed of myself for being white or for being a man.

And shame can come my way for reasons that I do not accept and in circumstances over which I have no control. I have no control over whether I am born with a visible disability. If I have a disability, that is nothing to be ashamed of. And I'll likely not accept (and certainly should not accept) the cultural norms that diminish my significance on account of my disability. But, the norms being as they are, I'll be diminished in communities that matter to me nevertheless.

And if my emotions are attuned to my reality, I'll feel the pain of being thus diminished. I'll feel shame even if I am not ashamed of myself for being disabled.

I can experience shame for reasons I do not accept and in circumstances over which I do have control. If the communities I care most about are deeply suspicious of the mainstream scientific encouragement to wear face coverings in public during a pandemic—if they think mask-wearing is an indication of inordinate fear and mindless subservience to government regulation—then I may experience shame when I am one of the few people to wear my mask in public. I will be diminished in the eyes of communities that matter to me when I am seen with my mask. Convinced as I am that masks are an effective way to mitigate the risk of spreading virus, I'll not be ashamed of myself. But I will be shamed. And if my emotions are attuned to the facts, I'll not only recognize that I've been socially discredited, I'll feel the sting of it. I'll have the painful emotion of shame.

Finally, shame can come my way for reasons that I accept and in circumstances over which I do have control. When I am caught engaging in activities that I know to be immoral and shameful, I will suffer social decline for reasons that I accept and for what I could have refrained from doing. I will be shamed. And I'll feel the sting of it. I'll feel shame. In this case, unlike the other three, I'll also likely be ashamed of myself.

The Rescue from Shame

In none of these cases will there be much I can do to mitigate my shame. I can't do anything about being white or disabled. And I can't desist from mask-wearing without violating my conscience. Even in the case where I suffer shame for having done something shameful, my shame is unlikely to be lifted even if I discontinue the shameful behavior. My low social standing will likely stick with me long after I've discontinued the shameful behavior that caused it. My low social standing may persist long after I've apologized, made reparation, and received forgiveness. Rescue from shame, recall, is not primarily a matter of forgiveness and reparation. It is a matter of restored honor. I can try to inoculate myself against the felt pain of the shame that has come my way. But that won't mitigate the shame. It'll simply render my emotional life insensitive to shame when it occurs. And, if I'm not careful, I may become shameless. I may become emotionally deaf to social discrediting when it happens to me—the kind of person who simply doesn't notice when they are losing connection and standing among respectable others.

The fact remains that felt shame is a destructive force. Countless are those who lose their grip on their sense of self because of the crippling effects of shame. Sometimes it's shame experienced in the wake of their own shameful mistakes. Sometimes it's shame experienced for reasons over which they have no control. Either way, the profound pain that comes with the experience of social discrediting robs them of self-respect—robs them of the ability to recognize and appreciate their own immeasurable worth. This is tragic.

For many, this descent into felt worthlessness has been successfully challenged by the contemporary attack on felt shame as an inherently toxic emotion. Insofar as people have avoided feeling worthless about themselves, there is much to be celebrated in this. It is not good or right for anyone, even those who've done the most despicable and shameful things, to feel they are worthless. Praise God for every person who is lifted from a feeling of worthlessness to a healthy sense of their own dignity!

But the wholesale denigration of felt shame is importantly misguided. The rescue from shame and felt shame is not ideally a function of inoculation against the latter any more than the rescue from the absence of companionship and felt loneliness is inoculation against felt loneliness. The remedy for felt loneliness is companionship. And the remedy for felt shame is honor.

A deep rescue from felt shame that has devolved into felt worthlessness, while it may involve some relief from the painful feeling of shame, will primarily be a matter of restoring honor. And, as we've seen, the restoration of your honor (once you have fallen into shame) is not typically something you can do for yourself. Both shame and honor are inherently social conditions. So the restoration of your honor is something you need done *for* you.

Being well-regarded in a community of respectable others, like companionship for those who are lonely, is a deep human need. If you're without it (or you think you're without it), the felt shame you experience may very well devolve into a feeling of worthlessness. But the root of the problem is not felt shame. The root of the problem is the *real or imagined social discredit* (the real or imagined loss of honor) that has caused you to feel shame. And the deep remedy is to restore your honor. But you cannot simply decide to be well-regarded in the company of respectable others. You need others to bring honor to you. This is not a problem you can solve on your own.

It takes a village (or, perhaps better, it has taken a village) to shame people with disabilities and victims of sexual abuse. And it will take a village to honor them. Shame and honor are social realities, and if we want to participate in the deep remedy for the shame-caused felt worthlessness of folks in these and other categories, we will take aim not primarily at their ability to feel shame but at the social norms and systems that give rise to their shame. We will find ways to honor the disabled—to lift them up into positions of visible power and influence. We will listen to and give an authoritative voice to victims of abuse. We will elevate those who have previously been marginalized. And we will recognize that this is not something that the marginalized are in a position to do for themselves. This responsibility will largely fall to those of us who have social capital to spare. Just as companionship must come as an offer from a willing other, honor must be conferred by someone in a position with significant social capital. To lift the shamed out of their condition, those in positions of social esteem will have to risk the perceived indignity of strong identification with the shamed.

And all of us, whether we have social capital to spare or not—whether or not, that is, we have a high social standing—are in a position to remind those around us that each and every person is loved and pursued by the God of the universe. The maker of heaven and earth is in a full sprint—robes and all—to embrace you, kiss you, put a ring on your finger, and throw a feast in your honor. Whatever the opinion of the company you keep, you are of immeasurable value to the One who matters most. You are so valuable that the God of the universe suffered the indignity of limited human form, betrayal, public humiliation, and naked crucifixion to rescue you from the shame of your condition, all to enjoy an eternal life of friendship and communion with you. And that's nothing to be ashamed of.

ACKNOWLEDGMENTS

This book has been a long time in the making. And my memory isn't what it used to be. So I know, even as I begin, that I'll likely neglect to mention things I've read or conversations I've had that have been enormously helpful. So I'd like to begin by thanking everyone who has had the patience to endure conversations with me about the painful topic of shame over the past several years or whose influence on this book is noticeable but unacknowledged. Conversations around "The Table" at Biola's Center for Christian Thought have been routinely helpful. As have the many conversations I've had with colleagues at Biola like David Ciocchi, Brad Christerson, Chris Grace, Liz and Todd Hall, Pete Hill, Adam Johnson, Evan Rosa, and Melissa Schubert, some of whom have read parts of the manuscript and have helped me along the way.

Thanks also to Andrew Bailey, Mary Bogan, and the rest of the "theology patio," Don Carr, Brian Forbes, Roger Freet, Josh Freeman, Dave Rhode, Gene and Judy Ten Elshof, Joanne Watt, Pete and Shelly Weiseth, and Jackson Wu for patient discussions as I've tried to sort through some of these ideas. Special thanks are owed to a small group of dear friends and fellow philosophers in the Southern California area for their friendship, encouragement, and helpful suggestions along the way: Jason Baehr, Tom Crisp, Kent Dunnington, Michael Pace, Steve Porter, and Dan Speak.

Thanks also to Madison Trammel and to Kim Tanner, Ryan Pazdur, and the rest of the editorial team at Zondervan for saving me from myself many times over and for helping to bring this project to completion.

NOTES

Chapter 3: Shame Everywhere

1. Bernard Williams, *Shame and Necessity* (Berkeley, California: University of California Press, 1993). See esp. chap. 4.
2. Williams, *Shame and Necessity*, 80.
3. Aristotle, *Rhetoric*, 2.6.
4. Aristotle, *Nicomachean Ethics*, 3.6.
5. Aristotle, *Nicomachean Ethics*, 4.1.
6. Aristotle, *Nicomachean Ethics*, 2.7.14.
7. Jessica Moss, "Shame, Pleasure, and the Divided Soul," *Oxford Studies in Ancient Philosophy*, volume 29 (Oxford: Oxford University Press, 2005), 137–70.
8. See *Summa Theologica* II–II, q. 144.
9. Here and in what follows, I am helped by Thomas Ryan, "Healthy Shame: An Interchange between Elspeth Probyn and Thomas Aquinas," *Australian eJournal of Theology*, 12, no. 1 (2008), http://aejt.com.au/__data/assets/pdf_file /0009/107469/Ryan_Practical_Theol_Conf.pdf.
10. John Locke, "Thoughts on Education," *The American Journal of Education* 13 (1863): 560.
11. See esp. Hume's "Treatise of Human Nature," book 2. Here and in what follows, I am helped by Paul Russell, "Hume

on Responsibility and Punishment," *Canadian Journal of Philosophy* 20, no. 4 (1990): 539–63.

12. For a more thorough discussion of the role of shame in Hume's conception of morality, see Annette Baier, "Moralism and Cruelty: Reflections on Hume and Kant," *Ethics* 103, no. 3 (1993): 436–57.

Chapter 4: The Case against Shame

1. Brené Brown, "The Power of Vulnerability," TED, June 2010, https://www.ted.com/talks/brene_brown_the_power_of_vulnerability?language=en.

Chapter 6: What Shame Is For

1. See Alan Downs, *The Velvet Rage: Overcoming the Pain of Growing up Gay in a Straight Man's World* (Boston, MA: Da Capo, 2005) or a short video series here: Alan Downs, "Alan Downs Speaks on Shame Based Trauma Pt 1," VelvetWarriors, April 30, 2011, YouTube video, 10:04, https://www.youtube.com/watch?v=Aj33c40f0-c.

2. Downs, *The Velvet Rage*.